YOUR
SHOW
OF
SHOWS

BOOKS BY TED SENNETT

Warner Brothers Presents
Lunatics and Lovers
Your Show of Shows

BOOKS EDITED BY TED SENNETT

The Movie Buff's Book
The Old-Time Radio Book
The Movie Buff's Book #2

YOUR SHOW OF SHOWS

Ted Sennett

MACMILLAN PUBLISHING CO., INC.

NEW YORK

Macmillan Publishing Co., Inc.
866 Third Avenue, New York, N.Y. 10022
Collier Macmillan Canada, Ltd.

Library of Congress Cataloging in Publication Data
Sennett, Ted
    Your show of shows.

    1. Your show of shows. I. Title.
PN1992.77.Y65S4   791.45'7   77-23104
ISBN 0-02-609710-9

Designed by Philip Grushkin

First Printing 1977

Printed in the United States of America

*For Bob, David
and Karen,
but above all,
for Roxane,
with love*

CONTENTS

*Photographs courtesy of Max Liebman, James Starbuck,
Bill Hayes, and the National Broadcasting Company*

ACKNOWLEDGMENTS

WRITING THIS BOOK was a labor of love, and the labor was made easier by the help of many people. I should like to thank the talented people who were associated with "Your Show of Shows" and who took the time to speak with me: Sid Caesar, Imogene Coca, Howard Morris, Lucille Kallen, Mel Tolkin, Tony Webster, James Starbuck, Frederick Fox, and Bill Hayes. I would also like to thank Julian Schlossberg and Millie Sherman for their comments, and my editor Bill Griffin for his faith and support. Thanks also to Barry Jacobsen for his great help.

Above all, I want to express my deepest gratitude to Max Liebman for making it all possible, and for making his kinescopes, photographs, scripts, and records of "Your Show of Shows" available to me. He is a wise and gentle man, as well as a consummate showman, and the long hours spent talking to him in his office were invaluable to me. I am also grateful to his delightful wife Sonia for her many kindnesses.

YOUR
SHOW
OF
SHOWS

1

Live from New York

DURING THE RUN of "Your Show of Shows," the program's press agent, David Tebet, now an NBC vice president, would turn up every week to see the show being blocked and watch the many pieces fall seamlessly into place. When he was finally asked why he continued to haunt the rehearsal halls, he replied: "I come over to the theater to see the miracle happen."

And it *was* a miracle, an electronic miracle unique in its day and not duplicated since. Every Saturday night, from February 25, 1950, to June 5, 1954 (with a hiatus every summer), an extraordinarily talented group of performers, writers, craftsmen, and technicians, under the aegis of showman Max Liebman, would culminate their grueling weeklong efforts by presenting ninety minutes of live, original, Broadway-caliber entertainment on television.

The key word is *live*. Without benefit of tape or canned laughter, supported by their formidable skills, their boundless energy, and their chutzpah, these people assembled before a living, breathing, *reacting* theater audience to bring them and the millions watching at home an hour and a half of comedy and music. There was no turning back, no leeway for slipups or boners, no room for sulking, temper tantrums, or hysterics. Timed to the second, the program had to move swiftly through its sketches, songs, and dances. Inevitably, there were last-minute changes, fluffed lines, or sudden gaps in the proceedings, but these were all handled with smooth professionalism.

The show was a sensational success. At a time when most television programming was innocuous or inane, "Your Show of Shows" appeared with its remarkable blend of bright, sophisticated comedy and top-caliber singing and dancing, its witty and irreverent style, and soon found a loyal audience. For many, Saturday night became synonymous with "Your Show of Shows," a time for deep and hearty laughter at the cavortings of Sid Caesar, Imogene Coca, and company. Indeed, my friends and I would wait happily for the "Stars Over Broadway" theme, and for that first nervous but endearing appearance by Sid Caesar to introduce the week's host or hostess. We would sit (or crouch or sprawl) before the flickering set in a joyful communion, cheering and applauding the best moments (of which there were many).

The performers on "Your Show of Shows" were gifted people, but it was Caesar and Coca who brought us back to the set week after week. For us, they were not only lovable, they were heroic. As a husband and wife engaged in (or on the verge of) continual warfare, as strangers sharing cliché opinions, as pantomimists caught in a variety of situations, they struck a responsive chord in all of us that echoed long after the program ended. They were also wondrously funny in their solo turns, Caesar as the brash and blustering oaf, Coca as the self-deluding but adorable waif.

Looking back across twenty-five years, we can see that Caesar, Coca, and "Your Show of Shows" were dispensing a form of entertainment that (we are told) is often received coldly by the public—satire, which holds up human vices and follies to ridicule and scorn. Boldly refusing to believe that audiences do not enjoy laughing at themselves, "Your Show of Shows" from the very first twitted, sniped at, and lightly mocked us all. Coming from a theatrical background where satire is often the order of the day, the program's writers laughed at our self-importance, our self-delusions, and our self-indulgence. Soon they expanded their satires of humanity into the specific realm of the movies. They took the movies' most familiar genres and most popular efforts, and accurately, hilariously, spoofed their styles and attitudes.

The critics loved it. And we loved it. We admired the skill that had gone into the creation. But we loved it because we sensed that, behind the sly malice, there was affection and respect for the source material, whether it was a recent movie or the perils and pitfalls of marriage. In the film spoofs, both American and foreign, we recognized the absurdity of many movie conventions and the pretensions of many moviemakers. In Charlie and Doris Hickenlooper, we recognized ourselves (or maybe our parents, friends, and neighbors). And every Saturday night, we laughed, faithfully and gratefully.

Of course, "Your Show of Shows" was not all comedy. From the start, the producer assumed that the audience could not only sit still for and even enjoy satire, but that it could appreciate first-rate singing and dancing. Instead of sandwiching an aria between the stand-up comedian and the dog act, the program showcased leading singers and dancers in well-staged excerpts from opera and ballet. Instead of flash-in-the-pan singers lip-synching their latest record, "Your Show of Shows" presented an ingratiating troupe of regular performers in song-and-dance interludes. Instead of a line of heavy-footed chorines, there were the imaginative dances of the lithe Hamilton Trio and the exotic Mata and Hari.

Before we describe how the program began, and how it was created, week after week, we should review its basic format for those too young to remember it, or those whose memories may have dimmed with time.

Following the signature song, "Stars Over Broadway," Sid Caesar would appear before the curtain to introduce the week's guest star. Clearly ill-at-ease (his nervous cough became a kind of trade-

Max Liebman with
press agent Dave Tebet.

2

mark), this heavy-set, handsome comedian would be mercifully brief as the guest star followed him onstage to present the first sketch. Most often this would be the "domestic" sketch involving Caesar and his co-star Imogene Coca as Charlie and Doris Hickenlooper, a married couple with wildly disparate attitudes toward practically everything. In their daily lives, small incidents would take on large significance; tiny disagreements would explode into full-scale warfare. There appeared to be a residue of affection between them, but theirs was clearly a marriage not made in heaven but perched midway between the higher and nether regions.

Usually, the domestic sketch would be followed by a musical number, perhaps an aria by Marguerite Piazza or Robert Merrill, or an imaginatively staged number performed by the Hamilton Trio or by Mata and Hari. The next segment would often involve Caesar and Coca in a clever pantomime (they were—and are —two of the best pantomimists extant), or in a sketch built on a series of clichés. Two passing strangers, they would meet to comment on the situation at hand (a wedding, a visit to the dentist, a graduation ceremony, etc.), taking bromides and twisting and shaping them into outrageous and hilarious forms that never seemed possible before.

Following a station break, there would often be a musical number styled for the company's resident young singers, Bill Hayes and Judy Johnson. This would usually be followed by a sketch prepared to showcase the week's special guest. (More often than not, this sketch was the weakest part of the program.)

After this, Caesar would frequently turn up in his familiar guise of the Professor, the shabby, Germanic, indomitably ignorant, self-proclaimed "expert" on a myriad of topics. Interviewed at the airport by reporter Carl Reiner (earlier, Tom Avera), he would use a dazzling array of ploys and evasions to keep from

responding to the questions and revealing his stupidity.

Following another musical number, perhaps the singing of the genial Billy Williams Quartette, or, later in the run, a beautifully staged number by dancers Bambi Lynn and Rod Alexander, "Your Show of Shows" would move to one of its weekly highlights: the movie satire. Possibly no feature of the program is recalled with greater delight, and with good reason. In these satires, all elements —writing, performing, direction—converged to create comedy material of a quality rare for television, even a quarter century later.

The satire might be directed at silent films, capturing the essence of these movies with affection and accuracy, or it might be aimed at the foreign films then achieving popularity in this country. Most often the satirical barbs struck closer to home: the most familiar American film genres and most popular recent movies from Hollywood.

Often, toward the end of "Your Show of Shows," the stage would be set for a solo by Imogene Coca. A comedienne of boundless artistry, she would turn up in various guises: as a would-be stripper teasingly wrapped in a long, shabby coat; a piquant twenties flapper; a croaking torch singer; or, most unforgettably, as a sweet and wistful tramp. Periodically, she would team with choreographer James Starbuck in splendid ballet excerpts tipped lightly in the direction of satire.

The next-to-closing segment of every program was a solo performance by Sid Caesar. Alone onstage, he would use his marvelously expressive face, nervous gestures, and rat-tat-tat speech patterns to limn a human being caught in the throes of living. Now blustering, then cajoling, at one moment a raging inferno, the next a bowl of Jell-O, Caesar created a memorably incisive portrait of a latter-day Everyman in these monologues.

The glow of the performances by Caesar and Coca would frequently extend into the show's finale, an elaborate production number that would sometimes involve the two stars. Here the full company would appear in a number built around a theme or a song, closing the week's program rousingly and in high style.

It all worked, beautifully and memorably, under the direction of Max Liebman. And it worked largely because Liebman refused to underestimate the intelligence of his audience. Writing in a Boston newspaper in 1950, he remarked, "One thing we take for granted on our show is that the mass audience we're trying to reach isn't a dumb one. It has a high quota of intelligence, and there's no need to play down to it. That is why we try to maintain a mature approach. We strive for adult entertainment, without compromise, and believe that the audience will understand it."

He was right. Twenty-seven years after its debut, "Your Show of Shows" is still warmly remembered. In this book, I have sought to recreate many of the program's highlights, to pay tribute to its joyous and, yes, significant contribution, not only to television, but to the entire history of the performing arts.

Miracles happen much too seldom to be dismissed. Let's see how this miracle happened, and why, so many years later, it remains indelible in our memory.

6

2

How It All Began

THE ORIGINS of any television program are always complex. Behind the official announcements, the hopeful pilot film, and the opening publicity salvos is an intricate web spun by many people: writers, television executives, sponsors, performers, and possibly some interested relatives and friends. Scattered along the way are assorted compromises, expediencies, and disappointments, as well as occasional moments of creative satisfaction and fulfillment.

For a television program as special as "Your Show of Shows," the process was no less complex. What it did have, however, was a gifted showman at its helm, an overseer with a firm and original concept of what could be attempted on the television screen. A man of consummate taste and great perspicacity, he applied the high standards he had developed over the years in the theater to the burgeoning medium of television. His name: Max Liebman.

A long time before "Your Show of Shows," he had started accumulating the vast amount of knowledge required to turn out live weekly music-and-comedy entertainment on the small screen. Born in Vienna, he had come to America at an early age and had plunged into the theater world as a writer and producer of vaudeville acts. For years he trailed along behind his performers, altering their lines, refining their routines, and quietly prodding them to improve. He also worked as a social director at summer resorts. Finally, in 1934, he came to an adult summer camp called Tamiment, located in Pennsylvania's Pocono Mountains.

Here, with the aid of an eager and talented group of budding performers and theater craftspeople, he created weekly original revues for the entertainment of fifteen hundred guests. His role was all-encompassing: he was the writer, the producer, and the director; he also supervised the costumes, scenery, lighting, and music, not to mention the cast. There was other entertainment during the week: a nightclub revue, vaudeville, movies. But like the nights to come on "Your Show of Shows," all efforts were concentrated on the major production every Saturday evening.

"For all that period of time before television," Liebman says, "I was really preparing myself for that medium at Tamiment. I was doing what you might call television without cameras. Our big show was Saturday night—one performance before a very tough audience. We had our own orchestra. Our own scenic department. Our own costume department. But until Sylvia Fine [Mrs. Danny Kaye] came in 1938, I was doing all the writing myself."

Liebman tells how he discovered Danny Kaye—for Tamiment and the world: "In the winter of 1938, Sylvia

Fine played with a little revue up in an attic someplace. She told me: 'There's a young fellow up there that you ought to go and see.' I did. I went up there and this fellow stepped out on the stage and before he opened his mouth, I said, 'That's it.' There was something very commanding about him. He attracted your attention immediately." Liebman signed Danny Kaye for his troupe at Tamiment.

Sid Caesar.

About the same time, Liebman also signed a genial sprite with a delicious sense of comedy—Imogene Coca. Encouraged by the enthusiastic response to the weekly Tamiment revue, he brought the best of the material to Broadway in the fall of 1939. Called *The Straw Hat Revue*, it ran for several months, providing a useful showcase for Coca, Kaye, and other talented Tamiment graduates. (Alfred Drake, not a Tamiment alumnus, was also in the cast, and the chorus included a young dancer named Jerome Robbins.)

Leaving Tamiment in 1940, Liebman joined forces with Sylvia Fine to put together an act for Danny Kaye. When Kaye was signed by Samuel Goldwyn, Liebman accompanied the couple (now married) to Hollywood, where they worked on Kaye's first feature film, *Up in Arms*. When it looked as though Kaye might go into the army, Liebman went to MGM as a writer. Occasionally, he returned to work with Sylvia Fine on Kaye's numbers in *The Kid from Brooklyn* and *The Inspector General*. During this time and afterward, he also served as a "play-doctor" to ailing scripts.

Liebman tells about his wartime discovery of Sid Caesar: "While I was on a hiatus from MGM, waiting for them to pick up my option, I got a call from Vernon Duke asking me whether I'd be interested in putting on a revue for the Coast Guard down in Florida in Palm Beach, called *Tars and Spars*. The intention was to do a recruiting show that would get people to enlist. The show's star was Victor Mature but there was a guy called Sid Caesar in it. We did a full-length revue down there, but when it went out on tour, it played in motion picture houses. We appeared at the Strand in New York, cut down to an hour. And that's when Sid and I concocted the airplane routine, which he repeated in the movie with Alfred Drake."

Several years later, Liebman worked

Imogene Coca on the Admiral Broadway Revue.

again with Caesar, helping him prepare his act for his crucial opening at New York's Copacabana. Caesar was an enormous success and became a leading attraction in nightclubs and vaudeville theaters, largely under Liebman's tutelage. Early in 1948, Caesar made his debut on the legitimate stage as one of the stars of the musical revue *Make Mine Manhattan.*

In the summer of 1948, Max Liebman returned to Tamiment in the Poconos. Aware of the burgeoning interest in television, he set about preparing a showcase for a program he had envisioned, one that would bring the style, approach, and techniques of the legitimate theater to television. As he tells it:

"At the time that television began to capture my attention, I realized that most of the programs being presented really originated in vaudeville and nightclubs or were an extension of radio. *My* emphasis was influenced, more or less, by the legitimate theater. There was a level of maturity and, if you will, an element of sophistication that was compatible with what I had done all my life before that. I wanted to bring this into the medium, without denigrating anything else. Good vaudeville is good vaudeville, and good cabaret is good cabaret. I felt that the one element that was not there was that of the legitimate theater: the element of sophistication.

"I don't mean the kind of sophistication which is over the heads of the audience. I'm referring to sophistication tempered by a sense of showmanship that brings the audience something they may not be as familiar with as they were in vaudeville—but something within their grasp to comprehend and appreciate. That's why, in the days when television sets were few, people in the Middle West would travel as far as fifty miles to the general store that had a set to see "Your Show of Shows" on Saturday night. They would write us fan letters mentioning how much they had enjoyed and appreciated the operas and ballets they had never seen before. It was *not* beyond their ken. The show was performed in a manner that didn't patronize these people."

But back in the summer of 1948, not many were persuaded that a live, sophisticated, Broadway-style revue was possible on television. On one fateful day, a talent agent from the William Morris Agency, Harry Kalcheim, brought an advertising agency man named Pat Weaver to the Poconos to see Liebman's Saturday night revue. Weaver had a client who was thinking about spending money in the new field of television. Liebman relates what happened:

"While Pat Weaver was having dinner, he said: 'I won't be able to stay after the show. I've got a long distance to go back.' But after the show he stayed up until four in the morning, talking to me.

The one thing he said was: 'Well, all right, I saw the show and it was very impressive. It is, I think, a good indication of what you could do in television. But on television you would have to do it every week.' So I said: 'Come again next week. And come the week after. And come the week after that.' He came back a few times and saw that it wasn't just a one-shot I was doing. And that was the beginning."

Weaver's original client dropped out, but then Harry Kalcheim interested Myron Kirk of the Kudner Agency (which handled Milton Berle) in the show. Impressed, Kirk offered the show to Admiral, a television manufacturer willing to take another cautious plunge into the uncharted waters of television (the year before, Admiral had sponsored a show starring Dean Martin and Jerry Lewis). Returning to New York, Liebman made a presentation that was brought to the president of Admiral. The president's decision was that the company would sponsor the show if (a large *if*) Liebman could bring it in as a one-hour program with singing, dancing, and comedy for no more than fifteen thousand dollars a week. This sum was to include scenery, costumes, writing, orchestra, actors, singers, and dancers. ("Today," Liebman points out, "we couldn't even get the orchestrations for fifteen thousand. Or the costumes.") The show was brought to Pat Weaver, still enthusiastic and now a vice president at NBC, in a strong position to act on his enthusiasm.

With Liebman as producer, the "Admiral Broadway Revue" premiered on January 28, 1949. The credits were virtually the same as those for "Your Show of Shows" over a year later: sketches by Mel Tolkin, Lucille Kallen, and Max Liebman; choreography by James Starbuck; settings by Frederick Fox; costumes by Paul du Pont, with the orchestra under the direction of Charles Sanford. Sid Caesar was listed as the star, with Mary McCarty (a hearty, broadly satiri-

Imogene Coca, choreographer James Starbuck, and Max Liebman.

cal comedienne), Imogene Coca, and the young dancing team of Marge and Gower Champion in support, along with a number of singing and dancing performers.

The format was largely the same as that of the revues Max Liebman had created at Tamiment: intimate sketches and songs, with solo turns for each of the leading players. Each of the nineteen shows revolved loosely around a theme: "Night Life in New York," "Cross Country," "Hollywood," "That's News," "Signs of Spring," "County Fair," etc. If some of the material was only vaguely related to the theme, no matter. The comedy, for perhaps the first time on television, was the smart, sophisticated humor of a Broadway revue. Television's devotion to broad comedy and the straight vaudeville format was toppled by the Admiral show. It dared to satirize modern painting, psychiatry, movie epics, advertising, and other themes not commonly treated on television.

Inevitably, some of the material was taken from the Tamiment revues. Imogene Coca, in particular, repeated a number of the successful routines she had performed there and even earlier in Leonard Sillman's *New Faces* revue: her hilarious mock-striptease, her modeling of many fur coats, her special version of the ballet, *Afternoon of a Faun*, and others. (These were later repeated on "Your Show of Shows.") Comedienne Mary McCarty, co-featured with Imogene Coca, performed many of the numbers she had perfected in nightclubs: her ode to Peter Lorre, her display of twenties "Flaming Youth," her Happy Hypochondriac, and her impression of that imbibing wine-taster, Miss Bubbles Winecellar of Giddy Heights, Indiana.

The Admiral revue was Sid Caesar's first exposure to television, and it turned out to be a major opportunity to hone his comedic gifts. His material throughout the nineteen-week run of the program included the routines that had first attracted attention to him: for example, the monologue from *Tars and Spars*, in which he acted all roles in a Hollywood aviation drama; his monologue expressing the thoughts of a penny gum machine; and his pantomime of a girl getting up in the morning. Other Caesar material looked ahead to "Your Show of Shows" and the characters and sketches he would refine and perfect on that program: the one-man version of a typical Technicolor Western or a familiar boxing movie, his impression of a shy and eager young boy at his first dance, and his satirical view of courtship through the ages. Here he also began the series of airport interviews with the world's self-styled experts, which reached manic heights of hilarity

on "Your Show of Shows." Among others, Caesar depicted Guiseppe Marinara, international film authority; Blubber Chinook, the world's greatest fisherman; and Sir Romley Buller-Groggs, the foremost swordsman of the day.

The talent was indisputably there: the satirical sense, the gift for dialects, and above all, the ability to portray a vulnerable human being beseiged by life's experiences. However, most of Caesar's material on the Admiral show now seems too diffuse, too vaguely focused for his very special ability. Later, on "Your Show of Shows," when he would stand alone onstage, grappling heroically with wife, children, or simple everyday events, the intensity of his confusion and even pain was brilliantly funny and touching. On the Admiral show, acting out courtship styles over the years, or a boy and girl on a date in different eras, he appeared to be reflecting the style of a comedian like Danny Kaye, another Liebman protégé.

Though they were often funny, the sketches on the Admiral revue suffered from the same diffuseness. They appeared to have been created not for television but for an intimate theater. Certain features turned up regularly; one was "Nonentities in the News," in which Tom Avera (an all-purpose actor who appeared for a while on "Your Show of Shows") interviewed Caesar, Coca, and McCarty in various guises: Esmerelda Cumquat, the Pie Queen of 1949; Gertrude Biddlehop, who bagged the biggest moose in history; Signor Ravioli, the world champion spaghetti eater. Other sketches offered variations on a theme: a pesky, obnoxious person discomfits and annoys another to the brink of insanity, i.e., Caesar as an indignant waiter in a restaurant, Coca as a maddening customer in a butcher shop. Still other sketches were satirically intended: the company principals as gruesome child stars; gaudily dressed ushers at the Radio City Music Hall, preparing to do battle with the moviegoers; Caesar as a rehearsing movie star slapped into insensibility by an overzealous actor.

Following the pattern that was later to be extended by "Your Show of Shows," the "Admiral Broadway Revue" also featured musical interludes, such as dance solos by Bobby Van and duets by Marge and Gower Champion, as well as elaborate musical finales that occasionally ventured into the new (for television) areas of ballet or opera. The first show presented "No, No, Rigolett," an opera performed in the style of a Broadway musical, and a delightful Tramp Ballet, featuring Sid Caesar and Imogene Coca as cavorting hoboes, was well received and was later repeated successfully on "Your Show of Shows." There were also musical finales built around the stories of Jesse James and Pocahontas.

If the "Admiral Broadway Revue" lacked the fine edge and the brilliant television sense of "Your Show of Shows," it still sounded a refreshing and innovative note for television during its nineteen-week run. The medium had seldom if ever presented comedy material quite so intelligent and sophisticated, or musical numbers quite so cleverly showcased.

The Admiral show (and its extension into "Your Show of Shows") was also responsible for important innovations in television itself, innovations that strongly influenced many programs that followed. It was the first television variety show with a permanent cast and permanent staff, including writers, a set designer, a choreographer, and a ballet corps. It opened WNBT's new International Theatre at Columbus Circle in New York City, the first theater expressly designed for television. It was the first television revue performed in the Broadway manner in a Broadway theater, with a full audience. It was the first television show to appear simultaneously on two major networks, being seen over the combined East-West Dumont network and on NBC stations in thirty-one cities. (The program was shown on kinescope to the rest of the country.)

Set designer Frederick Fox was responsible for significant innovations. Working under a severely limited budget, he was required to make the greatest

Below and on the following two pages, set designs by Frederick Fox.

Set designer Frederick Fox at work.

possible use of every piece of scenery, artfully transforming props and backdrops from show to show. For the first time in television, scenery was built, stored, repainted, and reused for a single program. The central piece was a large blue cyclorama set across the entire back of the stage. Against this background, Fox combined scenery pasted on canvas, cut-out props made of plywood, a few solid pieces of furniture, and projections on the cyclorama to create lifelike effects. The scenery was hung on very fine piano wire and would descend from the flies when required.

Another small revolution was wrought by Fox's lighting. Realizing that television was controlled by its technological minds, he persuaded the show's lighting staff to change their usual procedures. Taking a leaf from the theater, he asked them to use lighting as a servant of mood and style, rather than as the means for making everything onstage glaringly bright and clear. Colored gelatins were employed to heighten, reflect, or enhance what transpired, rather than revealing every person or object in sharp focus. The effect was most marked in the dance numbers; an intimacy with the viewing audience that television had long thought difficult or impossible was created.

Max Liebman has described the change

Innovative lighting enhances the mood of this
dance number by Bambi Lynn and Rod Alexander.

in this way: "Our first problem when we came into the International Theatre—which, by the way, two weeks before had harbored a stage play—was that we had to turn it into a television studio. The engineers were still involved in trying to get what they called 'as clean an image as possible.' They had no concept of depth or lighting moods. In other words, if a character stood in the foreground and there was a bookcase about twenty feet behind him, they wanted the lighting to reveal the titles on the books, more or less. There was no depth at all. They used scoop lighting—scoops were big containers for large incandescent white bulbs of five thousand watts that lit up the whole area being photographed. Well, we changed all that."

The reviews for the Admiral show were largely enthusiastic. John Crosby, in the *New York Herald-Tribune*, wrote: "For an hour's entertainment, I can't think of anything better in New York's expensive nightclubs. Come to think of it, there isn't anything much better on Broadway, either." He praised the show's "talented and extraordinarily energetic people." *Billboard* magazine exclaimed that "everybody concerned can take long, deep and repeated bows," praising the program's "sizzling pace, sustained interest, top performance, fine dancing, yock-producing comedy, and a production comparable to the top small musicals now playing the stem." *Time* magazine, in a long interview, said: "Its jokes and patter are brittle, rowdy, funny, and full of satirical references. . . . By and large, the costumes, décor, and choreography are better than may be found in any nightclub and many theatres."

The principal cast members were widely praised. *Time* noted that "Imogene Coca is just as funny modeling a moulting fur coat as she is imitating what Broadway columnists sometimes call a 'chantoosie.'" The reviewer also cited Mary McCarty as "a bouncy comedienne who can tear apart a popular song with

fine abandon or imitate a female wine-taster getting drunk on the job." The *New York Post* wrote that Sid Caesar was "forceful, versatile, and agile." *Billboard* also enthused that "Sid Caesar's double-talking and vocal sound effect abilities received full rein. . . . He was as great on TV as he's been in other branches of showbiz."

Singled out as the master showman behind the program, Max Liebman himself spoke to a New York *World-Telegram* reporter about the rewards of creating a weekly live revue for television:

Any Broadway actor will tell you that he's in the business because it's exciting as well as challenging. And it is! But look what we have on television. Whereas it takes months and months to put on a two-hour revue on Broadway, we do an original one-hour show, with singing, dancing, and comedy—in one week. Theatre die-hards speak of the thrill of opening night. Hell, we have one every week!

Despite the strong reviews, the Admiral show ran its appointed nineteen weeks and closed on June 3, 1949. The program had boosted Admiral's sales, and the company decided that the money allotted to the show could be put to better use by manufacturing more television sets. "They couldn't manufacture TV sets fast enough," Max Liebman says. "It wasn't the way they wanted to advertise them for the coming season, so they paid us off and now we were afloat."

At this point, Pat Weaver reentered the picture and spoke with Liebman about producing a new and extravagant television revue that would run for a massive two and a half hours. Liebman gulped and suggested that two and a half hours was too long, but that he would willingly take on a production that would last an hour and a half. An agreement was reached that the Liebman production, entitled "Your Show of Shows," would constitute the last ninety minutes of a program with the umbrella title "NBC

Saturday Night Revue." Comedian Jack Carter would head up the first hour in a more vaudeville-oriented program of comedy and music.

Liebman began to organize the new program, taking on many of the people who had worked with him on the Admiral Broadway Revue: Sid Caesar, Imogene Coca, Tom Avera (later replaced by Carl Reiner), and Howie Morris, a diminutive and vastly talented comedian who had appeared occasionally on the Admiral show; writers Mel Tolkin and Lucille Kallen; choreographer James Starbuck; set designer Frederick Fox; conductor Charles Sanford, and others.

Howard Morris and Carl Reiner in an antic mood.

Talented new people were added: opera stars Marguerite Piazza and Robert Merrill; singers Bill Hayes and Jack Russell, joined later by Judy Johnson; the Billy Williams Quartette, formerly known as the Charioteers; dancers Nelle Fisher and Jerry Ross; the dance team of Mata and Hari, which had worked with Liebman at Tamiment; and three brilliant and inventive dancers called the Hamilton Trio. Later, other regular performers would be added and some would be replaced.

From the first, the program differed from the Admiral show in several important respects. For one, it had a weekly host or hostess, usually a person well-known from films or the theater, who would introduce each number and who would also perform in a comedy sketch. (The host of the first two shows was Burgess Meredith, followed by Rex Harrison and then Melvyn Douglas.) For another, the program expanded the strictly comedy-and-popular music format of the Admiral show to include large segments of opera and ballet. The first show offered Robert Merrill and

Marguerite Piazza in an excerpt from *La Traviata*; the second had Merrill performing an aria from *Carmen*. (There was also a violin solo by Mischa Elman.) By the seventh show, Imogene Coca and James Starbuck danced an excerpt from a comic *Swan Lake*.

The most significant changes, however, were in the more skillful and imaginative use of cameras, and the much clearer awareness of the potentialities of television. No longer resembling a filmed intimate stage revue, the program made greater use of camera movement to catch Sid Caesar's bellows of rage or suffering, and Imogene Coca's infectious grin or lascivious wink. Where the Admiral show had occasionally seemed detached and precious, the sketches on "Your Show of Shows" brought the viewer in close to the action—Caesar and Coca, alone or together, in pantomime or sketches, expressing the most basic emotions in a way that made us all laugh heartily at them and at ourselves.

Originating from New York, "Your Show of Shows" premiered on February 25, 1950, as part of the "NBC Saturday Night Revue." (The Jack Carter hour came from Chicago, with a cast that included Cass Daley, Dorothy Claire, Benny Baker, and Donald Richards.) For the first time, the famous "Show of Shows" theme song was heard:

> Stars over Broadway
> See them glow.
> Get ready to take in
>   Your Show of Shows.
> Show of Shows! Show of Shows!
> Come on and step lightly
> And walk brightly,
> And join Broadway on parade.
> See that happy, fabulous throng
> Get their fill of rhythm and song. . . .

The first ninety-minute show included:

Singers Judy Johnson and Bill Hayes.

The opening number, "Stars Over Broadway."

"Main Street, U.S.A."—sung by Marguerite Piazza, danced by Nelle Fisher and Jerry Ross

"Life Versus Theatre," a takeoff on Noël Coward, with actress Gertrude Lawrence as the point of contention between husband and lover

Sid Caesar interviewed as Professor Kurt von Wolfgang, the famous psychologist

"Sweet Betsy from Pike"—sung by Bill Hayes, danced by Nelle Fisher and Jerry Ross

Imogene Coca expounding on the joys of "Smorgasbord"

A takeoff on the voyage of Christopher Columbus, with Sid Caesar as Columbus

"The Wiffenpoof Song," sung by Robert Merrill

Imogene Coca as turn-of-the-century musical star "Lillian Bustle"

Gertrude Lawrence singing "I Don't Know"

Sid Caesar in a monologue, "It'll Be Nice," as a man walking down the aisle to be married

A large-scale finale to "Dangerous Dan McGrew"

Though Jack Carter's segment of the "Saturday Night Revue" was largely dismissed, "Your Show of Shows" was received with generally ecstatic notices. Jack Gould in *The New York Times* called it "really out of the top drawer, boasting variety in the true sense of the word and having an adult flavor throughout. . . . The standout was Sid Caesar. . . . Since he started on television with the Admiral Broadway Revue, his comic

Marguerite Piazza and Jack Russell in an operatic excerpt.

artistry has matured enormously and he must now be ranked with the genuine clowns of the day ... NBC got off to a fine start, displaying both creative pep and style. The network can walk with its head up this morning, even on Madison Avenue." *Variety* hailed the program as "a solid block of big-time entertainment and sales potentials," also giving the larger share of praise to "Your Show of Shows": "That the show took on almost immediate added value with the New York origination wasn't surprising, with the Caesar-Coca contributions, some magnificent and imaginative overall dance production numbers and the overall pacing as the outstanding elements." (*Variety* liked the second show even more.)

The New York *Journal-American* singled out producer Max Liebman for praise: "He is clearly the top man in the TV musical field. He has given bright fluidity to the once static backgrounds, adds modern polish to ballet designed especially for television, and works with Sid Caesar on routines he once did with Danny Kaye and Betty Garrett and others during his Borscht Circuit period ... His fifteen years of dipping into entertainment borscht gives the program a definite flavor of experience, adaptability, and taste."

"Your Show of Shows" had been launched successfully as a witty and imaginative program that would permanently change the television viewing habits of the American public, extend the horizon of television in many felicitous ways, and crown the careers of two supremely talented artists named Sid Caesar and Imogene Coca. In time, it became a legend that this book hopes to recreate.

3

The Weekly Miracle

How *was* IT POSSIBLE to turn out a live, original, ninety-minute program of comedy and music every week? This was a question asked many times of Max Liebman, who would patiently offer the same response: "For each time I am asked, I have to ask myself. There *is* no formula, except that we have the best talent available in each capacity. What really counts is taste, style, experience, and, above all, showmanship." Still, there was the weekly challenge of creating fresh material, the enormous task of coordinating actors, singers, dancers, musicians, and production staffers into a cohesive, smoothly functioning company.

We can sense something of the dimension of Liebman's awesome job by describing the day-to-day efforts to put "Your Show of Shows" together. For the producer, it was a seven-day schedule that permitted no lapses, no wool-gather-

ing. It began on Sunday, with Liebman meeting with James Starbuck, the choreographer, and Aaron Levine, custodian of the music library, to work up new concepts for the following week's musical and production numbers. The meeting could take several hours or an entire day, but Levine seldom had a problem coming up with the music required by Starbuck for his numbers. "Levine's reserves are practically unlimited," Liebman noted at the time.

The working week really began on Monday, when the writers would convene to discuss ideas for the upcoming show, all derived from what Liebman called "over-the-weekend thinking." Lucille Kallen and Mel Tolkin, the versatile, Tamiment-trained duo who had written the "Admiral Broadway Revue" (they were superb lyricists and composers as well as comic writers), were the first writers on "Your Show of Shows," along with Liebman himself. (Sid Caesar, who was always present at the freewheeling creative sessions, never did any actual writing but contributed concepts and suggestions from his extraordinarily fertile comic mind. Imogene Coca would frequently attend these sessions as well.) Later in the program's run, they were joined by Tony Webster, a writer with a sharp wit and well-developed sense of the absurd—he had written for Henry Morgan's television show and for Bob and Ray—and by a brash and funny young man named Mel Brooks.* For a period during one season, the writing

---

* Max Liebman has described his first encounter with this now prominent and extraordinarily successful writer/director/actor: "I first met Mel at the old Broadhurst Theatre—Caesar had brought him. Sid introduced us and said to Brooks: 'Do for Max what you just did for me.' And this, believe it or not, is what Mel did: He faced the empty seats and sang; 'Hello, hello, hello/I've come to start the show/ I'll sing a little, dance a little/ I'll do this and I'll do that/ And though I'm not much on looks/ Please love Mel Brooks!' Whereupon, he got down on one knee and made a Mammy-type gesture."

James Starbuck, the choreographer.

*Aaron Levine, custodian
of the music library.*

staff also included two fast-rising brothers, Neil ("Doc") and Danny Simon.

To create the week's comedy material, the writers would disperse to various offices, to work singly or in pairs.* (Only the domestic or "Hickenlooper" sketch would have been actually assigned the previous Friday.) Ideas, situations, and lines would be tossed back and forth; most would be rejected and a few would be accepted and pursued. Throughout the writing sessions, the volatile focal point was Sid Caesar. In a *Theatre Arts*

* Lucille Kallen has described the first office set aside for the writers: "We were in a rather seedy part of the city, and there was very little space. So Mel and I got the boys' dressing room, the dancers' dressing room. So we sat there surrounded by jock straps, if you please. That's where we worked or else we squatted in the hallway."

article in May, 1953, Max Liebman described the process:

An idea tentatively tossed into the air can be fatally impaled in mid-flight by a grunt from Caesar, or it can soar up on his pleased grin and return to earth shaped into a storm, peopled and costumed. Let Miss Coca suggest, say, that there ought to be a skit about a couple on a bus, and that afternoon it is in rehearsal. Here is the strength I counted on at the outset, this unity of understanding and the easy interchange of comedy values. We are richer nowhere than in our department of comedy, nor speedier.

When a comedy script was decided on, the sketch was "put on its feet" under Liebman's direction. Caesar and Coca were sufficiently familiar with it to make their own contributions during a period of improvisation. The writers were summoned, and it was here that the sessions could turn hectic and stormy as temperaments clashed and nerves became frayed. The pace was frenetic but it was exhilarating. As Lucille Kallen described it: "To command attention, I'd have to stand on a desk and wave my red sweater. Sid boomed, Tolkin intoned, Reiner trumpeted, and Brooks, well, Mel imitated everything from a rabbinical student to the white whale of *Moby Dick* thrashing about on the floor with six harpoons sticking in his back. Let's say that gentility was never a noticeable part of our working lives. Max Liebman was fond of quoting what I think was a Goldwynism: 'From a polite conference comes a polite movie.' "

Never noted for politeness, Mel Brooks was the most undisciplined of the writers. He was notorious for arriving long after

Sid Caesar with writers Mel Tolkin, Lucille Kallen, and Mel Brooks.

the work had begun, shouting something in the nature of "Lindy has landed!" and rushing out shortly afterward, leaving several genuinely funny ideas for sketch material. On more than one occasion, an exasperated Max Liebman threw a lighted cigar at him. (Today, he remarks genially that "I was sufficiently angry to throw a lighted cigar but not so much to hurt him.") Brooks himself recalls those feverish sessions: "Everyone pitched lines at Sid. Jokes would be changed fifty times. We'd take an eight-minute sketch and rewrite it in eight minutes. Then Sid and Coca and Reiner and Morris would relearn it from scratch. On Saturday night, it had its first and only test—before twenty million people."

From all the shouting, laughter, spitballs, and half-eaten sandwiches emerged some of the best, most sharply honed comedy television would ever see. And though the weekly writing sessions were hardly an unalloyed joy, the years with "Your Show of Shows" are recalled with pleasure by the writers. Lucille Kallen remarks: "It was a lot of fun. Can you imagine being young and single and at the top of the heap and writing for guest stars like Rex Harrison?" And Tony Webster notes: "For me, and I'm sure for all the other people, it was really exciting. The people were all talented and it was a perfect example of everyone contributing. It was a case of all the right people being in the right place at the same time. All very bright and talented."

Mel Tolkin's sentiments are similar: "We were too young to know it's impossible. It was all new, we were all poor, and that's an important part of it. The biggest miracle was the combination of people. It was quite accidental, like any miracle. I think that with one writer different, it wouldn't have been the same show. Or with one actor different." Tolkin also comments on the writers' aversion to straight "gags": "We didn't write gags. We didn't think in terms of gags. We were almost a little snobbish about it."

At the same time that the writers were working on the comedy material, all other departments were getting under way. On the four complete floors of space in a building on Manhattan's West Fifty-sixth Street, there were special studios or offices for each group involved in the production: stars, musicians, writers, singers, dancers, etc.

On Monday afternoon, Liebman would confer with scene designer Frederick Fox and costume designer Paul du Pont concerning the sets and wardrobe requirements for the week's show.

On Tuesday, full rehearsals would start. James Starbuck would begin to work on the intricate dance and production numbers. Clay Warnick would assemble his choral group for intensive practice. Frequently, the singers and dancers would be brought together for close integration of their vocal and ballet routines.

After lunch, the guest star would arrive, usually eager to begin rehearsal. (Many prominent personalities, after the

Starbuck directing dancers Frederic Franklin, Pauline Goddard, and Wallace Siebert.

Rehearsal break.

success of the program, *requested* a guest booking.) Frequently the star would be more game than experienced in the ways of television, having come from the legitimate stage, motion pictures, the ballet, opera, or some other medium. The sketch would be discussed and set in motion, giving the guest a fast if rudimentary course in the television revue.

Wednesday and Thursday were given over to hard work as the pace accelerated. Groups would be rehearsing on every floor of the building. While the players performed the sketches and the dancers and singers carried out their numbers to piano accompaniment, Max Liebman would roam from floor to floor, checking on the progress of the various units and

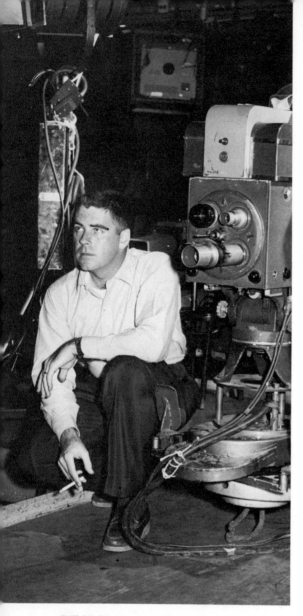

Bill Hobin, camera director.

discarding items which seemed to be repetitive or dull. He would now begin work on the split-second timing and running order of the show. At the same time, scenery would be constructed, costumes would be created by a small army of tailors and seamstresses, and furniture and other properties would be gathered from shops and galleries throughout the city.

For the writers, Wednesdays were devoted to sharpening the final scripts for the sketches. In informal sessions, the writers would take notes and make the last changes in the material. The dialogue of the sketches would be turned over to the secretaries for mimeographing. The cast would begin to memorize its lines.

On Wednesday evenings, Liebman would also meet with key members of the production staff to discuss the musical material for the following Saturday show, ten days ahead. After dinner, he would listen to music and recordings collected by the untiring musical researcher, Aaron Levine, and select numbers for that show. Scores of selections would be carefully analyzed and considered.

On Thursday, the company would work with the mimeographed script, to which additions were made in different-colored pages. Rehearsals would continue through the day in all departments. Sketches and specialty material would be sharpened or even drastically changed, if necessary. In the music department, the copyists would frequently remain until morning, turning out the parts to be printed for the twenty-five-piece orchestra. (For special production numbers the orchestra could be augmented by as many as fourteen additional players.)

On Friday morning, Liebman, Caesar, and the writers would meet to discuss possible sketch or comedy material for the following week's show. Then, after lunch, the entire company would assemble for the first time since beginning rehearsals to go through a "dry run" of the complete show (performed in the rehearsal hall without cameras, costumes, or scenery). At this time, camera director Bill Hobin and NBC's technical director, who would be pushing the buttons according to Hobin's directions in the control room the next day, would observe the show in its rough form and take notes.

Max Liebman wrote in *Theatre Arts* about this dry run:

The dry run is usually without dismaying incident. We have edited out the unacceptable during the earlier rehearsals and made all necessary adjustments. The dry run allows us to revise the running order, time the numbers, and arrange movement for the most effective use of the camera. Sometimes, but not often, we may find that a number considered irresistible all week is not only resistible but downright bad. This produces a major crisis, which is promptly referred to the writers who specialize in crises.

In the legitimate theater on Broadway, the dry run is often the most trying time —tempers flare and nerves jangle as the result of four or five weeks of pent-up feeling. But "Your Show of Shows" was locked into a rigid schedule for one busy week, so these feelings had little or no time to fester, and the program's dry run was usually free of excessive strain.

After the dry run, the orchestra, which had rehearsed in the ballet room that morning under Charles Sanford's direction, would appear at the theater at 4:00 P.M. for a run-through of *all* the orchestra music that was being used in the sketches and musical numbers. The or-

Heino Ripp, technical director.

chestra rehearsed at the theater with the singers, dancers, and anyone else who had musical cues, and this run-through would not be repeated until 5:00 P.M. the next day, at the dress rehearsal. "We didn't use music that was played on the Hit Parade," Liebman notes. "We used mostly show music."

Following the orchestra rehearsal, there was a technical run-through with the stagehands, primarily to indicate where the scenery should be placed. "We would begin to 'hang' the show and put everything in its place," Liebman recalls. "Friday night was the night for scenery." Hanging the scenery was no perfunctory task. In his *Theatre Arts* article, Liebman wrote: "The deft manipulation of scenery is all important in television in that it serves that ogre, the time factor. Sometimes a changed order of the show, established by the dry run, requires an alteration in Frederick Fox's scenery placements."* Working in the control room, Bill Hobin and his staff would line up their camera shots for the actual performance.

On Saturday, at 8:00 in the morning, the entire company would meet at the theater for a day-long camera rehearsal. Following a rigid schedule prepared in advance, each item in the show would be carefully "blocked" before the cameras. Only painstaking planning and minute attention to detail made it possible to block so complex and elaborate a show in one short camera day.

Liebman recalls that occasionally there were problems of his own devising. He would be fully satisfied with camera directions for a musical number, only to have a dancer surprise him with a movement of such breathtaking grace that he would discard the whole picture concept

---

* The show's vast collection of scenery, valued at nearly one million dollars, was stored in a warehouse separate from the headquarters on Fifty-sixth Street; no other NBC program had access to the scenery, costumes, or musical arrangements of "Your Show of Shows."

Charles Sanford rehearsing the orchestra.

to re-create a proper setting for this moment of beauty. A superlative but unplanned moment of comedy could drive him to the same indulgence.

At 5:30 P.M., a full dress rehearsal would get under way. With a secretary, Liebman would watch the rehearsal on a monitor, dictating notes but never interrupting as the show proceeded to its conclusion. He would be seeing the show exactly as it would be viewed several

hours later in millions of homes across the country. Following the dress rehearsal, Charles Sanford and his orchestra would continue working until only a few minutes before the show was scheduled to go on the air.

At approximately 6:30, the entire cast and crew would be assembled for a final exchange of notes and ideas. There would be notes from the choreographer to his dancers, from the choral director to his

singers, from the camera director to his crew, and from Liebman to people in every department. Adjustments would be made. Sometimes, in an extreme situation, a sketch would be discarded, and an old sketch substituted. A kinescope of the old sketch would be sent for and quickly reviewed. ("It was always my theory," Liebman says, "that it's better to do an old thing that's good than a new thing that's bad.")

At 8:55, Liebman and his staff were in the control room, ready to begin. His recollections of that critical moment are still vivid: "When the clock showed exactly nine o'clock, the show went on the air. The world could have caved in, and I wouldn't notice. I was as cold as ice. Nothing touched me because we had done everything we could—except for the one thing that couldn't be done until the actual performance. And that was

Rehearsing the "Love Thy Martian" sketch.

In the control room: Heino Ripp, technical director; Bill Hobin, camera director; Max Liebman, producer; Marcia Kuyper, Hobin's assistant.

Sid Caesar rehearsing a monologue.

The cast and staff: On the floor, from left to right: Clay Warnick, choral director; Paul DuPont, costumes; James Starbuck, choreographer; Charles Sanford, orchestra conductor. First row: Lucille Kallen, Mel Brooks; unknown; Carl Reiner, Imogene Coca, Max Leibman, Sid Caesar, Tony Webster, Mel Tolkin, the Billy Williams Quartette. Second row: fifth from left, Irvin Kostal, music arranger; seventh from left, Jack Russell, singer; Howard Morris, Judy Johnson; Bill Hayes; the Hamilton Trio; Rod Alexander; Bambi Lynn. Third row: singers and dancers. Absent when the photograph was taken: Mata and Hari, Marguerite Piazza, Robert Merrill.

the gap in the timing between the dress rehearsal and the actual show.

"Now the audience began to adjust the timing by the way they received the show. Laughter took up time. We had to adjust to the laughter. We couldn't break into the laughter or the performers wouldn't be heard. We had to make constant adjustments in each half-hour to come out on the nose. Messages would go to the conductor: pick up ten seconds, or spread ten seconds. With actors it's difficult to speed up or pad. I was in constant communication with the stage manager backstage. The control room was like the headquarters of a battlefield. We had all kinds of safety devices. At the end of the show, it was easy. We

Bill Hayes and Robert Merrill singing an excerpt from Faust.

had announcements of upcoming shows, institutional announcements."

"When something unexpected happened, we were in trouble," Liebman remarks. But, he adds, "the trouble was often funny." There were times when Caesar and Coca were required to improvise during the course of a sketch, and their quick thinking sometimes resulted in hilarious moments. During a satirical take-off on the then-popular film *From Here to Eternity*, Caesar was doused repeatedly with buckets of water during a spoofed version of the passionate beach scene. When an unusually large bucket of water was tossed at his head, he ad-libbed: "Rough night, isn't it?" The audience roared with laughter, and even Coca, the unflappable professional, suppressed a giggle by burying her face in Caesar's shoulder.

Over the years, the show faced many vicissitudes endemic to a company under the continual tension of performing live on the air. Each week was a new baptism under fire as the members learned and grew and sharpened their skills. Under the experienced eye of Max Liebman, who had survived similar fire through his years at Tamiment and elsewhere, the performers were "learning on the big time" and learning fast. It was, for all of them, an exhilarating and matchless experience.

And the laughter they received was spontaneous, not coaxed from a machine created to regulate the sound of ghostly recorded laughter. Liebman recalls: "The thing that told us whether it was a good show or a bad show was the response of the audience in its laughter. Frankly, I pressed the button for 'Applause' in the production numbers. But I couldn't press a button marked 'Laugh' because there *was* no such button!"

For one hundred and sixty performances, through triumphs and traumas, the miracle occurred every week.

And leading the triumphs with Imogene Coca, and sometimes causing the traumas, was Sid Caesar....

4

Hail, Caesar!

For all the brilliance of the stock company of players on "Your Show of Shows" over its four-year run on television, there is no denying that its reigning comic figure was Sid Caesar. As the master showman who controlled all aspects of the program, Max Liebman had brought together a gifted group of performers. But early on, as the civilian director of a Coast Guard revue called *Tars and Spars*, he had recognized a special spark of genius in Caesar, and he had helped to keep that spark glowing until, on "Your Show of Shows," it burst into flame. He had recognized that behind the nervous cough, the ill-at-ease demeanor, and the fullback's physique was an enormously talented comedian. Millions of television viewers learned what Liebman already knew: that Caesar's expressions of joy, rage, insecurity, and pain were mirror reflections of all of us.

At the peak of Caesar's popularity, Liebman described this talent astutely: "Caesar tells no jokes and elicits terrific crescendos of mirth. Characterization,

not gags, is the main ingredient of his technique. He is blessed with a kind of magic truth, the uncanny ability to project the core and humanity of the character he is playing. Beneath the surface humor there is a wry commentary on the conventions and hypocrisies of life."

Many years later, Liebman reflected on Caesar's rare quality: "Sid could never be a stand-up, one-line comedian. In fact, he didn't like one-line jokes in the sketches because he felt that if the joke was a good one, anybody could do it. One-liners would take him away from whatever it was that drove him into his completely personal approach to comedy. He wanted to do things only the way *he* could, and this is the drive that governs any artist, any creative person. A painter wants to paint in his own way, and that's why so many are recognized by what they paint. That's why distinctive musicians, composers, and writers want to be recognized by that personal thing they bring to their work that nobody else does. And I used to say that Caesar insisted on instinctively 'Caesarizing' his material. His material was sifted through a sieve that was purely personal. No matter how it went in, it came out as Caesar."

During the first year of "Your Show of Shows," Caesar did not go unappreciated by the critics. In the New York *Herald-Tribune* of September 19, 1950, John Crosby wrote: "Sid Caesar is one of the wonders of this modern electronic age. Where all the other comics are moaning about the tremendous drain television exerts on material, Caesar has more genuinely funny comedy sequences than he knows what to do with in a week." A day earlier, Jack Gould in *The New York Times* wrote: "There can no longer be the slightest doubt that Sid is not only a star but a star for whom television alone is entitled to take major credit.... Through his own patience and the guidance of Max Liebman, Mr. Caesar has steadily matured in his art.... As long as Mr. Caesar is around, 'Your Show of

Shows' is not to be missed." An article in *TV Guide* in April, 1950, asserted that "Mr. Caesar needs no insult routines, stale gags, shabby sketches to garner his laughs. In his comedy approach he has found the greatest source of humor to be people themselves. . . . He is a clown of majesty, the big attraction on 'Your Show of Shows.' "

Inevitably, the question arises: how did a stocky, ambitious young saxophonist from Yonkers become television's "clown of majesty"? Caesar's background provides faint clues but no real explanation.

Born on May 8, 1922, Sid was the youngest of three sons of Austrian-Polish immigrants. His father was the proprietor of the St. Clair Lunch, a restaurant where Sid, as a young teenager, worked with his brothers, often as bouncers for overly boisterous customers. Here, among the international clientele of Polish, Russian, and Italian construction workers, Sid

began to absorb and accumulate his repertoire of intonations, accents, and dialects. (Where he picked up the ability to play a whitewall tire, a slot machine, a seltzer bottle, and a cattle stampede remains a mystery.) The Caesars lived over the restaurant and rented rooms to transients.

At Benjamin Franklin Junior High School, and later at Hawthorne Junior High School, sturdy young Sid, hoping to avoid fights, took up weight lifting to develop muscles everyone had to respect. At Yonkers High School, he concentrated on learning to play the saxophone rather than on his studies. While still a Yonkers student, he played with Mike Cifichello's Swingtime Six for about two dollars a night. (They played from "nine P.M. until unconscious.")

After graduating from high school in 1939, Sid searched for a musician's job in Manhattan, without success. To fill the six-months residence requirement for joining the musicians' union, he finally took a fifteen-dollar-a-week job as an usher at the Capitol Theatre, using the money to study the saxophone and clarinet at night. His goal was to make a classical instrument of the saxophone through studying at the Paris Conservatory. ("I was a real longhair," he recalls.) Meanwhile, he was promoted to doorman at the theater, at a smashing eighteen dollars a week. He remembers: "When the cold weather came along, they promoted me to doorman. A wonderful break, heh? I had a clear view of the crowds going into Lindy's but my own lunches were brought to me by my mother, who carried hot soup and sandwiches all the way from Yonkers."

Eventually, he managed to get work with some of the leading bands of the day, including those of Charlie Spivak, Claude Thornhill, and Shep Fields. With the outbreak of World War II, a musical career seemed highly remote, and in November, 1942, Caesar enlisted in the Coast Guard. But not before he had received his baptism into the world of comedy. Before joining the Guard, he had worked in a band at the Avon Lodge in the Catskills, where he also assisted comedian Jackie Michaels in his routines. The crude pie-in-the-face (or more accurately, tomato-in-the-face) slapstick turned him off the obvious gag forever. At the Avon Lodge, he also met Florence Levy, who became his wife in 1943.

In the Coast Guard, Caesar was alerted to go overseas, and his outfit was equipped with full field packs, gas masks, and helmets. Following a big sendoff, they embarked—to Manhattan Beach in Brooklyn! Caesar spent a year guarding Brooklyn's docks and delousing German prisoners of war. He also played saxophone in the base orchestra, and during the breaks, he amused his fellow sidemen with impromptu monologues, foreign-language double-talk, and satirical portraits of their officers. He also continued to practice comedy routines and wrote

sketches for a Coast Guard revue called *Six On, Twelve Off*.

Caesar came to the attention of composer Vernon Duke (then a lieutenant in the Coast Guard) who had been ordered to put together a recruiting show in Palm Beach, Florida. The show was called *Tars and Spars*, and Max Liebman was asked to be the civilian director. Attracted by Caesar's budding comic prowess, Liebman worked with him to develop the routine that became an important stepping-stone to success: the spoof of Hollywood's wartime Air Force movies. In this routine, Caesar played all the roles, including the airplane. The hero is "Smiling Jim"—he smiles relentlessly through thick, thin, and enemy strafing—who knocks out his friend Bill and takes his place in a dangerous mission. (Bill regains consciousness and shouts at his reckless friend: "You fool, you! Come down! There's no propeller on it!") In a hilarious dogfight between Jim and a German aviator, Caesar points up the contrast between the planes: "American planes always sound so *cute*. German planes are so *mean*." But nothing daunts heroic Jim as he sacrificially heads for a crash with the German plane. But a second later, "Jim is alone in the sky..." This spoof was a popular feature in *Tars and Spars* and was later used in both the

A catnap between rehearsals.

Admiral revue and "Your Show of Shows."

After a national tour in an abbreviated version that played movie houses, the revue was filmed in Hollywood by Columbia. Or more accurately, the studio turned out a minor musical that used the name of the revue, Caesar's airplane routine, and nothing else. Released early in 1946, it starred Alfred Drake, who had worked with Max Liebman in *The Straw Hat Revue* but was famous as the original Curley in Rodgers and Hammerstein's *Oklahoma!* Janet Blair, Columbia's resident soubrette, played opposite him in a mild mélange of comedy and music. As a character named Chuck Enders, Caesar was the movie's featured comedian and won the best notices. *The New York Times,* while recognizing the considerable influence of "J. Durante and D. Kaye," found Caesar the only promising performer and called his movie lampoon "vastly amusing."

The New York Daily News called him "a real comedy find," adding that "his interpretation of an Air Force movie is alone worth the price of admission."

After leaving the Coast Guard, Caesar remained in Hollywood for a while with a Columbia contract, but appeared in only one film, *The Guilt of Janet Ames.* A turgid psychological drama starring Rosalind Russell and Melvyn Douglas, this movie was released quietly and died with scant notice. Caesar appeared briefly as a nightclub comic who burlesques psychiatrists and psychoanalysis. (Apparently the producers didn't notice —or didn't care—that he was spoofing the very movie he was appearing in. As Caesar tells it: "I thought they would cut it out of the movie, but they didn't. They let it ride.")

Unused and untried in Hollywood, Caesar returned to New York to begin playing the circuit of nightclubs and variety stages, attracting attention at the

Sid Caesar in the "Christopher Columbus" sketch on the first "Show of Shows," February 25, 1950.

Copacabana and the Roxy Theatre. (Until he appeared at the Copa, he had never been in a nightclub in his life.) Max Liebman recalls that Caesar appeared at his home one evening to tell him about his engagement at the club. Liebman asked him: "What are you going to do?" "The airplane routine," he replied. "And what else?" "That's why I'm here." Together, they worked out an act that drew enthusiastic reviews.

While playing at the Roxy, one of New York City's last golden movie palaces, Caesar was seen by restaurant proprietor Leo Lindy, who raved about him to producer Max Gordon. Gordon saw Caesar and, in turn, recommended him to producer Joseph Hyman, then casting a stage revue called *Make Mine Manhattan*. He hired Caesar for the revue, an attractive and well-received show that opened on January 15, 1948, at the Broadhurst Theatre. The cast included David Burns, Kyle MacDonnell, Sheila Bond, and Joshua Shelley. Directed by Max Liebman, the sketches spoofed, among other things, the bizarre menus of Schraffts restaurants, filmmaking in New York, and the city's noisy civil servants. Caesar was featured prominently, performing his monologue as a penny-gum machine, playing several United Nations delegates, and dancing a soft-shoe with David Burns in "The Good Old Days." He received the 1948 Donaldson Award for the best debut performance in a Broadway musical. *Make Mine Manhattan* closed on January 9, 1949, after a year's successful run, just in time for Caesar to open in the "Admiral Broadway Revue" on television the following month.

These were Caesar's origins, but they can hardly explain the communion of a comedian and a television camera that began with the Admiral revue and reached its spectacular peak on "Your Show of Shows." Over the course of the program, Caesar participated enthusiastically in all of the material, appearing in sketches and duologues with Imogene

Coca, in specialty numbers, and in elaborate production numbers. Yet alone onstage, with his entire physical being intensely involved in a specific situation, he was at his most riveting, his most remarkable.

The shining essence of his humanity emerged most clearly in those moments when he portrayed a comic Hamlet offering a monologue to the world. With a face that could express various degrees of happiness, fear, loathing, dismay, surprise, and desperation, Caesar solo could dredge from his own experiences, from his own psyche, the basic emotions and attitudes of every person in his audience and turn them into an awesome, hilarious torrent of words. In the throes of one of his monologues, Caesar was like a man possessed, reaching for the inner being of the perennially anxious, hopeful, exasperated character he was playing.

And he *did* create a character in his series of monologues. Somehow a man emerged whose odyssey could be traced from show to show. From the young man

terrified at the thought of proposing marriage, to the young married coping with jobs, children, and in-laws, to the proud middle-aged father watching his son graduate from medical school or his daughter being married, Caesar offered an amazingly perceptive and uproarious portrait of Everyman in the middle of the twentieth century. Though physically a large man (as the series progressed, he gained considerable weight), he was able to express the longings and the hang-ups of the little man buffeted by life. The small frustrations we all experience were expanded to manic proportions in Caesar's masterful monologues.

As a young man in love, he begins by contemplating that traumatic experience: a proposal of marriage. A mountain of indecision, he wavers between assertive action and terror at having to "take the plunge":

I've got a right to be married! I've got a right to get married! What right have I got to get married? Sure, I've got a right

...I'll go over and propose to her, but I can't just go over like that ... I've got to have everything right so she'll be sure to say yes. ...

Getting "everything right," however, inevitably leads him to changing his mind, and even a prepared romantic speech becomes a disavowal:

I've got to make her feel that she's somebody, that I respect her, that I look up to her. ... I'll say to her ... Doris, you are a queen, and I am a tiny twinkling star. You are the soft breeze floating over the vast ocean and I am but a pebble on the beach. ... You are everything ... life itself, and I am nothing. [Pause] So you better get somebody else because I'm no good for you. ...

Yet somehow he gets through the proposal, only to face a second obstacle: breaking the news to his parents. Here his ramblings are those of a classically intimidated son, tied to his mother with an umbilical cord of steel and saddled with an emasculated father. When he reminds his mother that she has already met Doris, his remarks are comic, but they also reverberate with a bitter-tinged truth:

Mom, what do you mean you don't know her? Don't you remember I introduced you to her? Took her over to the house and said: "Doris, this is mother. Mom, this is Doris." And Doris said: "How do you do?" And you said: "You're stealing my boy. I brought him up, I washed him, I cleaned him, I fed him, I held him in my arms, and now that he's starting to look like something, you're stealing him from me! I hate you! I hate you!" Now it's because of little things like that, she doesn't like to come over here so often....

He objects vehemently to being treated like a baby, claiming that he has nightmares about being called "baby boy."

("Sometimes the nightmares are so violent I fall out of my crib.") Starting tomorrow, he's going to feed himself. He also has to cope with a father whose voice he hasn't heard in ten years. ("Pop, what do you say? Mom, let Poppa talk. What do you say, Pop? Mom, *please* let Poppa talk.")

Apparently, he gets their reluctant blessing because we next see him marching down the aisle, expressing the happiness, confusion, and severe doubts of any about-to-be groom. His pleasure may have a touch of desperation about it ("I'm *glad* I'm getting married! This is the happiest day of my life!"), but he manages to contemplate a serene and settled future as a married man:

It'll be nice. Get up in the morning, no more running down to some one-arm joint and grabbing a glass of orange juice and coffee.... No, sir. Eat like a man.

Put my robe over my pajamas. Get into my slippers. Walk into the kitchen. Yes, looking for somebody? Oh, it's you, darling. I didn't recognize you. [A look of shock and horror comes over his face.]

Finally, overcome by the sentiment of sharing a blanket with his wife, or getting up for a crying baby, he begins to whimper, then cry as everyone around him dissolves in happy tears. "Do I promise to take her to be my lawfully wedded wife? I do, I do." And he walks off, sobbing with joy.

Each man's odyssey as a husband and father has its rewards and tribulations, and over the span of "Your Show of Shows," Caesar's monologues managed to touch on the most recognizable of them. Incisively etched by the writers, brilliantly spoken by Caesar, these monologues expressed the vagaries of most marriages. Consider the beleaguered husband's words as he storms into a friend's house after an argument with his wife:

It's finished! I'm telling you, it's finished! It's all over.... It's no use.... She's a nice woman, she's a fine woman, she's a lovely woman ... but she's a miserable wife!

Claiming to be a reasonable, easygoing man at the end of his tether, Caesar pours out his tale of woe—and the portrait he draws of his less-than-ideal wife would give a stronger man pause. She refuses to have towels in the house ("It's getting so that I take a shower with a raincoat on"), she insists on sitting on the phone all day ("One day I had to make a phone call, so I said to her, 'Get off that phone and sit on the chair!'"), and she is inclined to be sarcastic in the most alarming fashion. When he complains of heartburn, she gives him a curious drink:

I said: "What is it?" She said: "Drink it, never mind." I said: "Tell me what it is." So then she gets sarcastic.... "It's poison ... that's what it is." ... So I don't want to argue with her ... I drank it. The

next thing I knew I was rolling around in agony.... I said: "What was it? What did you give me?" She said: "I told you ... Poison!" That's one of her little tricks. She was only playing a joke....

Still, Caesar's marriage has its rewarding moments, depicted with a wry and observant humor that makes them linger in the memory. The story of Snow White, related to a drowsy child, becomes mixed with the dire events of the father's day: "So the wicked stepmother sent one of her huntsmen into the forest to kill Snow White but Snow White had a partner Larry who doesn't know how to take an inventory. So Snow White was stuck with an order that she couldn't get rid of as long as she lives...." The traumatic event of taking a son to school for the first time becomes a lesson that veers abruptly from "Don't cheat" to "Cheat cleverly": "When it comes to exams, don't take from others, don't peek over somebody's shoulders at the next desk. Don't take from others. Put it on your own cuff, then cover it with your sleeve. Nobody knows, nobody sees."

A firm and strong parent? Certainly, with perhaps one slight exception, as he tells his son's principal:

Now the boy is a normal, healthy child. We've raised him to be an upright and well-disciplined boy. On most things he does not have his own way—only once in a while, just so he doesn't have any complexes. You have to give in to the child just a little. So on one important detail he has his way ... I let him carry a knife. Of course, I dulled it and took the point off so it isn't dangerous.... So please humor him because remember, he's armed....

Years later, the same son is about to become a doctor, and at the graduation ceremony, the father, though consumed with pride, is not unaware of certain problems and limitations. He remembers his son's childhood: "He was sensitive . . . always daydreaming . . . a delicate, sensitive boy. The least thing, and he'd take it to heart. I mean I'd go over to his bed in the morning and say [shouts]: 'Get out of bed, you lazy bum! Do something!' And he'd faint . . . A very sensitive boy. . . ." And when the son decides to marry before finishing his medical studies, he tries (unsuccessfully) to talk sensibly to the girl: "First, he must get his degree, so why not at least postpone the idea of marriage and leave him alone, and if I see you cross the street to my house, I'll run you over." But even though the marriage took place, Daddy remains undaunted: "There's my son's wife. I'll get her yet. Four times I tried, but she's slippery."

The marriage of a daughter is yet another traumatic event in this man's life, and he faces it with the usual mixture of delight and exasperation. He falls into a rage when he discovers that the groom's family has invited forty-eight guests ("Together with our family circle it'll be six hundred and forty-eight!"), and he balks at the caterer's black caviar, vichyssoise, champagne, and pink ice shaped like a swan ("Listen. Make six hundred and forty-eight bologna sandwiches on thick bread. I don't want them to go away hungry."). From his daughter, he seeks reassurance that she really loves the guy ("If you're not sure, sit down and start eating those six hundred and forty-eight sandwiches, 'cause I'm not throwing out any money for nothing.").

And how does Our Hero react to the timeless problem of mother vs. daughter-in-law? With the usual forthright candor that conceals a lily-livered coward. When his mother complains bitterly about his wife, he defends her in his own fashion: "What? She doesn't know how to keep house? So she's not formal. That's relaxed living. That's the new thing. She doesn't use plates . . . so it's a little difficult when it comes to eating. You gotta go like that [makes gesture of scoop-

ing]." When his mother accuses him of being a milquetoast, he is quick to deny the charge: "Now you're *really* wrong. I'm the boss in this house. She listens to everything I say. . . . Oh, no? When you walked in that time and we were fighting, I told her before you came in: 'Darling, go over, pick up that vase, and hit me over the head with it.' . . ."

Apart from the normal turbulences of marriage, the man Caesar projected in his monologues had to cope with his own human frailties, with the fact that as he grew older, his poundage increased while his hair decreased. In his musings on these familiar infirmities, Caesar became the comic spokesman for all aging, balding men. Staring in the merciless mirror, he becomes resolved to do something about what he sees:

Look how chubby I am . . . look at my ears, how fat they are. My eyeballs don't even fit in their sockets any more. And look at this jacket. It used to be a top coat. . . . Yep, today's the day I'm gonna do it. . . . Today's the day I'm going on a diet. . . . I gotta have will power . . . I gotta be strong . . . and you gotta have a lot of strength. . . . So make me a big breakfast 'cause I gotta have a lot of strength to go with this diet! . . .

Through the long day, he tries desperately to hold onto his waning will power: "Be strong, be strong. You made up your mind. . . . You gotta take the bull by the horns and cut him up and make big steaks with mashed potatoes and gravy!" Finally, he opens the refrigerator, sees the food, and emits a heart-rending scream: "I'll go on a diet tomorrow. I promise. I'll go on a diet tomorrow. Meantime, I'll heat up the stove and get the broiler going. . . ."

An even more devastating experience is his discovery of falling hair. Caesar masterfully ranges across a variety of emotions as he contemplates a future of baldness. He begins by bemoaning his fate: "Heredity! It's all my father's fault.

Because of my father, I'm going bald. When I was a kid, my father got mad, he used to hit me in the head and he loosened my hair. Now it's falling out!" He tries to convince himself that it's all for the best—baldness will change his whole personality and he'll become an intellectual with dignity: "People will treat me with respect. Strangers will come up to me and ask me questions: 'Hey, Baldy, which way to Ebbet's Field?' And I'll say: 'You continue down this street—what do you mean, *Baldy?*' . . ." He also considers fleeing to other countries, but grimly foresees himself being addressed as "Monsieur Baldon" and "Señor Baldini."

Caesar's Man of the Monologues has a strong streak of sentiment for the past, even if it's only for the memory of his beautiful shock of hair ("I used to comb it back . . . I could hardly see where I was going. . . . My friends used to call me 'Sheila.' . . ."). When he attends the reunion of his graduating class, he can cast an nostalgic haze over events that may not have been exactly wonderful: "We had a fine football team. Princeton can have its tiger mascot. Yale can have its bulldog. Navy can have its goat. Army can have its mule, but we're proud of our Cranbury Rat. He used to scare the whole stadium."

His recollection of the school's "Magnolia Walk" falls somewhat short of Busby Berkeley: "I remember those nights strolling down the walk, strumming on my uke. Those big moonlit nights looking over the river. All the guys had the same line. You could hear it all over the place. They all kept saying, 'Gee, I wish we had some girls in the college.' . . ."

Nevertheless, those were happy days, and his eyes become misty as he sees the welcoming banner. "Welcome back, Class of '28. Twenty-eight of the nicest fellows you ever want to meet. Kind of lonesome at the college that year."

Over the run of "Your Show of Shows," Caesar's monologues placed him in a large number of familiar situations, from all of which he emerged shaken but relatively confident. He went through the agony of asking for a raise; the anguish of not finding his wife at home as usual —and suspecting the worst; the irritation of coping with a repulsive brother-in-law. And he contended with simpler matters: trying to get to sleep; taking his family for a Sunday drive; cheering up a sick friend; coping with a bad cold; buying a new suit. On one occasion, he was a man who took his unbridled love for his antique car ("a 1922 Rio Rita") into undreamed-of heights of ecstasy: "My baby, my car, my everything. Now I'll just take these blankets off the car here and just remove the cellophane wrapping. Always keep my car in cellophane and a layer of absorbent cotton."

Sometimes Caesar's monologues took him into the realm of fantasy, where his skill at mimicry was as sharply honed as it was in the workaday world. At various times, he portrayed a newborn baby, a penny gum machine (the routine he had done in *Make Mine Manhattan*), and a dog, who, not surprisingly, turned out to have the same frustrations, aggressions, and jealousies as any human: "There's my own food—mush. How do you like that? We must be having guests tonight. They don't give me meat all day. They starve me so I'll break my neck tonight doing tricks so I can get a little piece of meat. Some psychology!" He was even able to enter the mind of a common housefly with what one can only surmise is remarkable accuracy:

What a house! My house! I was so lucky to find this house! Always something to eat. Crumbs on the table, banana peels on the floor, lettuce leaves in the sink . . . what a nice, sloppy house! Well, I'm hungry. [Discovers they've cleaned up the house] They cleaned up the house! It's disgusting! They're expecting guests! How do you like that! Nothing to eat in the house! . . . Why should I aggravate

The Professor being interviewed by reporter Carl Reiner.

myself? So I'll eat out today! It won't kill me. But I hate restaurants. That greasy food! I can't stand greasy food! I keep slipping off!

Caesar brought to these monologues the ferocity and bluster of a man besieged by life but unwilling to admit it. The same comic intensity characterized another familiar guise of Caesar's on "Your Show of Shows": the Professor, that self-styled expert on a variety of topics, whose airport interviews with a baffled but persistent roving reporter

(Tom Avera, later Carl Reiner) were frequent inducements to laughter on the program. (This character had first appeared on the Admiral show but reached the peak of lunacy on "Your Show of Shows.")

The Professor (his title was sometimes Doctor) was a gentleman of Germanic origin but dubious credentials whose clothing—rumpled frock coat, battered top hat, tacky vest, shabby tie—would have qualified him more for a tramp's convention than for an institution of learning. He was dauntless in his ignorance. Professing to have an intensive knowledge of his field, he would resort to any shameless trick to keep his interviewer in a state of confusion: spitting out non sequiturs like broken teeth, launching anecdotes that ended somewhere on the other side of madness, breaking into Germanic-sounding doggerel, coughing and wheezing mightily to conceal his abysmal stupidity. The Professor was, in fact, a broad lampoon of every pontificating authority who had ever bored a captive audience with his punditry. (In his approach, there were unmistakable intimations of writer Mel Brooks' hilarious "Two-Thousand-Year-Old Man," popular a number of years later. Not coincidentally, Carl Reiner, who interviewed the Professor for most of the run of "Your Show of Shows," was also Brooks' reporter, again trying to stay cool and collected as he talked with the still-sprightly senior citizen.)

Was there any area of scholastic endeavor or human activity that was too difficult, too challenging for the Professor? Hardly, and he tackled every area with unswerving enthusiasm and the complete objectivity of a blank mind. For example, as Dr. Sigfried von Sedative, authoritative author of *Wake Up and Sleep*, he goes briskly to the point:

REINER: *Doctor, would you explain to the audience in simple language the basis for your theory on sleep?*

CAESAR: *Sleep is wonderful. Sleep is beautiful. But sleep is no good if you're wide awake.*

For the insomniac, Dr. von Sedative offers a remarkable remedy that deserves to be recorded in its entirety:

Well, first of all, flop into bed. Don't sneak into bed, flop. And then you relax all the parts of the body. Say good night,

The Professor being interviewed by reporter Burgess Meredith.

toes, shhh. Quiet, go to sleep. And soon the toes drop off. And then you say, ankles, shh, go to sleep, ankles, the toes are sleeping and the ankles fall asleep. And then you say to the knees, all right, put on the sleeping caps, go to sleep. And they fall asleep. And soon the whole leg is asleep. And you say to the stomach, all right, stop the mixing, it's time to go to sleep, put away the tools. Toora ... loora ... loora.... And then the arms go to sleep. And the chest, all right, stop breathing, beddy bye, and the throat, stop swallowing, don't talk no more, good night. Then the brain, go to sleep, good night. Will you go to sleep, will you go to sleep? Come on now. Now stop that and go to sleep. What's the matter with you? My brain is out of its mind.... Shh. You'll wake up everybody. Look, the toes are awake. Look, toes, go to sleep. Fall asleep, toes. Shhh.... Now will you stop that? ... Now wait.... What are you, a wise guy? All right, everybody up. I'll show you. Some day you're gonna wanna sleep. I'll walk the body all night.*

In one sketch, Professor Sigmund von Fraidy Katz, an authority on mountain climbing and author of *Mountain Climbing: What Do You Need It For?*, enters with a rope around his waist, looks at the end of the rope and says, sadly: "What a sweet guy!"

REINER: *You look preoccupied.*

CAESAR: *Hans Goodfellow. I always said: "Hans, you don't climb a mountain on roller skates." But he was always starting something new. He was a sweet guy.*

Asked about the greatest mountain climber of all time, the Professor responds with alacrity:

* Mel Brooks has said that this sketch provoked the only "real fistfight" he ever had with Caesar. Caesar didn't want to do the sketch, and they battled down Fifty-fourth Street. Caesar finally conceded, and the sketch was included in the show, very successfully. Brooks' comment: "I remember it in vivid detail. You don't face death that often, so I remember it well."

CAESAR: *Jim Richardson. He was the greatest. He made the record, you know. He climbed the Matterhorn in two weeks, four days, and twelve hours.*

REINER: *Is that the record?*

CAESAR: *No, he made the record on the way down. Ten seconds. He was a sweet guy.*

REINER: *You still save that rope as a token of your great respect for Hans Goodfellow?*

CAESAR: *No. If I didn't have the rope, my pants would fall down.*

Professor von Fraidy Katz proffers his advice on what to do in an emergency. If, for example, your rope breaks:

CAESAR: *Well, as soon as you see the rope breaking ... scream and keep screaming all the way down ... this way they'll know where to find you.*

REINER: *But, Professor, isn't there anything else you can do?*

CAESAR: *Well, there's the other method. As soon as the rope breaks, you spread your arms and begin to fly.*

REINER: *But humans can't fly.*

CAESAR: *How do you know? You might be the first one. Anyway, you can always go back to screaming. That's always working for you.*

REINER: *Was Hans a flyer or a screamer?*

CAESAR: *He was a flying screamer and a crasher, too.*

On other subjects, the Professor is equally erudite. Listen, for example, to the distinguished expert, Dr. Rudolf von Rudder, author of *You Too Can Fly*, as he explains how an airplane gets off the ground:

Well, it's a simple theory ... matter is lighter than air. You see, the motors, they pull the plane forward and they cause a draft and then it taxis faster down the field and the motors go faster and the whole plane vibrates, and then when there's enough of a draft and a vacuum created, the plane rises off the runway into the air, and from then on it's a miracle . . . I don't know what keeps it up.

Authority though he is, Dr. von Rudder is not without a sense of the high drama of aeronautics. Asked to relate the most daring feat of aeronautics he has ever witnessed, the doctor tells about the legendary Pierre Le Prop, who believed that anyone could fly without a plane and with only a few adjustments to his body. The Academy of Aeronautics laughed at him, called him crazy. "I'm crazy?" Le Prop said. "I'll prove to you I'm not crazy." He goes to the top of a mountain on which a castle stands. He perches on top of the castle with a piece of canvas between his arms and a little propeller on his head, as the scientists shout: "You're crazy! You're crazy!"

REINER: *He must have been killed.*

CAESAR: *No, he wasn't so crazy. He didn't jump.*

And what is Dr. von Rudder's final word on aeronautics? "Fly . . . Fly any place . . . anywhere, but always remember one thing. When you're flying, keep one foot on the ground."

Moving with agility from flying to food, the Professor, now named Kurt von Stuffer, author of *Food Can Be Habit-Forming*, becomes suddenly knowledgeable on the subject of nutrition. The essence of his theory on food? "My theory is never—never—eat on an empty stomach. Always take a bite before you sit down to eat." He also comments on the familiar dictum that "you are what you eat":

CAESAR: *When a person eats fluffy eats, little cakes, pasty and fancy little things, then that person is also fluffy. But when you eat meats and strong, heavy food,*

The many faces of Sid Caesar.

then you are *also* a strong person. *I had a patient once who was so fluffy, so light, that I prescribed a diet of meats and strong foods, and in a couple of months the patient was six feet tall with muscles and a big, flowing moustache.*

REINER: *That's wonderful.*

CAESAR: *No, that's terrible. She was a woman and her husband didn't like it.*

His most interesting case?:

They brought me a patient. It was a terrible sight. I examined him and found out this patient couldn't take any strong foods like meat. He was thin, emaciated, small—weighed twelve pounds. So I examined him and found out why. He was just a baby. He was born yesterday.

While the Professor is prone to deal with such weighty subjects as medicine and high finance, he is just as knowledgeable in the areas that Drs. Joyce Brothers and Rose Franzblau tackle so fearlessly. In fact, his knowledge of human behavior, of romance, courtship and child rearing, has every bit as much depth and perception as theirs. Asked by the interviewer how one can recognize the symptoms of "love at first sight," Professor Ludwig von Hartflopper, author of *Love: Its Cure and Prevention,* replies sagely:

Well, you're walking along the street, and you see a beautiful girl. Right away your eyes get the message and you say, oh, what a beauty! Then your eyes send a message to the brain, and the brain goes wow . . . and the brain right away sends a message to the heart and the heart goes boom boom, and the heart gives a message to the pulse, and the pulse goes "Get that girl!" . . .

When all the parts of the body respond, they tell the feet: "Go after her!" The feet start walking, and the brain tells the tongue: "Say something," and the tongue says: "Hello, miss, isn't it a nice day?" Unfortunately, the girl's eyes send a message to her brain, and the brain says: "Smack him! He's a masher!"

Nevertheless, if love should lead to marriage, one could always consult Dr. Heinrich von Heartburn, who wrote *Happy Though Married.* Asked if having the same interests makes for a better marriage, he replies without hesitation (the Professor may evade, equivocate, and ignore, but he never hesitates):

Oh, certainly, of course. This is very important if you marry an intelligent girl. You've got to keep up with her. If she goes to the opera, you go. If she goes to a concert, you go. If she goes to a lecture, you go. If she reads a complex technical book, you read it. You must keep up with her. And so if you want to be smart, marry a stupid woman.

Dr. von Heartburn's marriage counseling is rather unorthodox, though perhaps not much different from the advice offered in *The Total Woman.* How do you keep a marriage healthy?

Make it interesting. Keep it alive. I showed a friend of mine once how to keep his marriage exciting. You know what he used to do? One day he'd come home from work, his wife would open the door, he's a French soldier, and he comes walking in. [Hums "Le Marseillaise"] The next day he's a policeman, he comes in, he starts to run around with the handcuffs and the badges, and the next day, he don't come through the door, he jumps through the window, he's a clown. He somersaults all over the living room and throws his wife all around the place.

Merely as an afterthought, the good doctor reports: "She left him. He was a maniac."

On the ever-popular subject of children, Dr. Ludwig von Pablum, whose book, *Children Are People, Only Smaller,* must have plumeted instantly to the bottom of the remainder shelf, summons up a few opinions that have a certain degree of sense. The interviewer remarks that children go through various stages and inquires: "At what age would you say a child gives his parents the most pleasure?" Dr. von Pablum's answer: "I'd say around twenty-eight. They're working. They're out of the house, they're sending money home, and what other pleasure is there in life?"

Plunging ahead gamely, the intrepid interviewer asks Dr. von Pablum to describe the psychological makeup of a child:

CAESAR: *Well, you see, in the makeup of girls the subconscious is always in conflict with the conscious and the ego cannot regard any of the involuntary reflexes which are happening in the present state, the past state, and the future state that cannot be comprehended. And that's the makeup of little girls.*

REINER: *And what are little boys made of?*

CAESAR: *Snakes and snails and puppy dog tails. That's what little boys are made of.*

For a wide-ranging authority like the Professor, it is not much of a leap from the tangled web of human relations to the tinseled world of show business, and he turns up on one program as Professor Kurt von Closeup, the distinguished producer and director who has written *My Life as a Director or: How to Live on $22.50 a Week.*

In a single interview, the writers succeed in demolishing scores of misguided, pretentious, and basically ignorant moviemakers. Reporter Carl Reiner makes a lengthy and complex statement on the art of the motion picture: "They have developed certain qualities peculiar to motion pictures, such as scope, plasticity, and a freedom from the element of the passage of time. . . . Would you care to comment on that?" he asks Professor von Closeup. "No," the Professor replies. "I'm mixed up already. I don't know what you're talking about." In a snipe at the movies' tendency to misinterpret a classic work of literature, von Closeup describes

"the biggest picture" he ever made: "I built a whole city and a castle and cleared a whole field and rented a forest and then you should have seen them—thousands of soldiers on beautiful horses, charging the castle with spears in their hands. . . . What a battle scene! What a picture!"

The name of the film: *Huckleberry Finn.*

Or mocking the perennial search for "new talent," the Professor describes a memorable incident in his career.

I was at that time in New York. I was shaving on the fifth floor of my apartment when I suddenly hear a voice outside: "Watermelon, watermelon, melon, melon!" I hear this wonderful, unusual voice: "Watermelon, watermelon!" Right away I get excited. I never hear such a voice in my own town of Vienna. I run over right away to the window. I look down and I shout: "Hey, you! Yes, you, the one who's shouting 'Watermelon.' What's your name?" And he said: "My name's Joe," and I said: "Joe, bring me up a watermelon." And it was wonderful. No pits.

One of the funniest interviews in the series took Caesar out of his German professor role and had him playing one Lemuel Cornball, the foremost exponent of rural and folk music. With a twang that makes Tennessee Ernie Ford seem like Laurence Olivier, Cornball takes every opportunity to turn every answer into an amazing string of bucolic references:

ANNOUNCER: *Mr. Cornball, I bet you enjoyed your airplane trip. Was it fun?*

CAESAR: *We was flyin' higher'n faster than a bald-headed eagle swoopin' down on a scraggly-tailed, black-hearted, chicken-killin' dead-eyed buzzard, protectin' her young in the month of November.*

ANNOUNCER: *That's interesting, Mr. Corn-*

ball. How does the noise and excitement of the big city affect you?

CAESAR: *I'm having more trouble sleepin' than a gray-eyed possum fleein' from the hungry, saliva-filled jaws of bayin' hounds in the black swamp on a foggy night in the middle of the month of July.*

Not surprisingly, Lemuel is also a composer. His latest opus? It's called "I'll Love You Till the Rope on the Old Well Bucket Disentwines Its Sacred Knot, Leavin' the Old Bucket Skip and Sink Beneath the Still Cool Waters of the Old Well in the Month of May."

Mel Brooks' influence on the Professor's interviews is evident throughout, but perhaps most conspicuous in the ramblings of Professor Filthy von Lucre, the financial expert who wrote *Money Talks, So Listen!* Asked to comment on the medium of exchange in prehistoric times, Professor von Lucre asserts that rocks were used by the cave men because they were scarce. ("It was the ice age. Plenty of ice cubes, but no rocks.")

If you wanted a nice two-room cave, it would cost you about six boulders, eight rocks, and twenty-four pebbles. A nice dinosaur steak was eight rocks and six pebbles, and if you were really well off you could get a nice six-room cave with an adjoining lake for about seven boulders, eight rocks, and no pebbles.

There were counterfeiters in those days, crooked cave men who would mix clay and cement and paint it to look like a rock. (They were called "rocketeers," of course.) Von Lucre tells of one fellow whose game was to stand in front of his cave and make faces at people passing by until they threw rocks at him. He became a millionaire and flourished until the crash—when the mountain fell down. "With rocks all over the place, there was inflation." Professor von Lucre informs us that fish became the new medium of exchange: "In those days you could really tell a rich man ... you could

smell him a mile away. But they had to do away with fish as currency. It was very impractical. Nobody would work in the bank."

REINER: *How is that, Professor?*

CAESAR: *You think the government is going to take rocks and fish? They want the cash, boy!*

And so it went most weeks, the Professor barking and thrashing his way through a series of interviews that made one forever suspicious of all the pundits, interpreters, and soothsayers who appear regularly in the nation's media. The interviews also made good use of Caesar's ability to zero in on a familiar type: the man who conceals his ignorance and insecurity under two dozen bushels of bravado and bluster.

Here, for the record, are some of the other eminent authorities portrayed by Caesar:

Professor Ludwig von Fossill, expert on archaeology, author of *Archaeology for Everyone or: Don't Lift Heavy Rocks.*

Professor Hugo von Gezuntheit, medical authority and author of *The Human Body and How to Avoid It.*

Professor Ludwig von Complex, authority on animal behavior, author of *Animals, Their Habits, Habitat, and Haberdashery.*

Professor von Muscle, the sports "maven," author of *Watch Your Body, Buddy.*

Professor Lapse von Memory, the memory expert, and author of *I Remember Mama—But I Forget Papa.*

Mad? Yes, but with the madness that makes us laugh at erudition gone berserk, just as Caesar's Man of the Monologues made us laugh at earnest human endeavor turned manic through the pressures of daily living.

5

Bravo, Coca!

How to describe the special glories of Imogene Coca? The offstage Coca has been called an extraordinarily shy and timid woman, fearful of riding in taxicabs through heavy traffic, distrustful of trains and airplanes, uncomfortable in crowded elevators. She claims to be intimidated by modern inventions of all kinds, and she has never tried driving an automobile. On "Your Show of Shows," her stage fright never diminished over the four years, and she could hardly get herself to view the kinescopes. Her modesty, though clearly unwarranted, is very real.

No matter. The onstage Coca is an assured artist, totally in control of her performance. The critics of "Your Show of Shows" were fond of calling her an elf, a pixie, a sprite, and indeed she is a tiny (five foot three) woman who looked even tinier beside the towering (six foot two) Caesar. But concentrated within that small frame was a virtual lifetime of theater experience, a sense of timing and of the *right* gesture developed over long, grueling, and often unrewarding years touring vaudeville houses and playing in short-lived revues and musicals. She had learned her craft and had never forgotten a single lesson.

The offstage Coca was (and is) a private person. Onstage in "Your Show of Shows," she was many persons, each of them sifted through her comic awareness of their all-too-human absurdity and fallibility. She was invariably gentle with her creations but never sentimental, laughing at their (and her own) posturings and pretensions without demolishing their humanity. As a housewife with a continual grievance against her husband, as a French chanteuse in the throes of passionate abandon, as a music hall soubrette of the twenties, or as a cheerful singing-and-dancing tramp, she inspired a kind of laughter all too rare in the cynical seventies: laughter without cruelty.

Like Caesar, she has a miraculously expressive face that can register every variety and shading of emotion, and on "Your Show of Shows," she was called on to register them all. In an article in *Life* magazine, Ernest Havemann described it eloquently:

On stage Miss Coca does strange, unexpected and in a way wholly lamentable things with her face. Her nose sags like an overwarm candle into utter dejection, or it jumps and quivers in imitation of a haughty dowager who has just been accused of cheating at canasta. Her chin expands and juts forward in fierce self-righteousness or sometimes just gets tired and vanishes altogether, leaving her looking like a cartoon-strip librarian. Her left eyelid can droop into the lewdest wink ever allowed on television and her right eyebrow can shoot up an eighth of an inch into the most innocent kind of moronic bafflement.*

This is the face of the clown, but like the best clowns, Coca adds a touch of poignancy to the buffoonery. Even at her

* "Girl With a Rubber Face," *Life*, February 5, 1951, p. 54.

most ridiculous—sprinting bow-legged into the arms of her ballet partner, huskily bellowing a torch song in mock-chanteuse style, or coyly confronting a burlesque audience in a shabby, ankle-length coat—she seems more than a mite vulnerable. She is the cheerful but not very beautiful girl at the party who wins over the boys with her charm and her eagerness to please. She touches the heart at the very moment she is tickling the funnybone. The program's choreographer, James Starbuck, has described this rueful quality: "There is a substance, a kind of glow about her on the stage—a Chaplinesque quality, an air of poignancy and sadness over the laughter." Of course, this is most evident in her inimitable tramp routines, where her jaunty and wistful style and her sweetness in the face of adversity suggest, without slavishly imitating, the genius of Chaplin's Tramp.

Unlike Caesar, Coca did not emerge from a conventional background. She was born into a theatrical family, the daughter of Joseph Coca, orchestra leader at the Chestnut Street Opera House in Philadelphia, and Sadie Brady, who, at an early age, was a vaudeville performer regularly sawed in half by Thurston the

Magician. Her father, a proud, brash, salty-tongued man, liked to gamble, and he would occasionally lose the band's entire Saturday payroll between the bank and the theater. Imogene (full name: Imogene Fernandez de Coca) was an only child, soon absorbed into her parents' world. She began piano lessons at five, singing lessons at six, dancing lessons at seven, and she was a full-time trouper at age fourteen. (She always preferred dancing, though she says that her family wanted her to study the violin.)

In the early years, she played variety houses all over New York, performing tap and ballet routines. She made her legitimate debut on Broadway playing a chorus girl in a short-lived revue called *When You Smile*, then spent the next five years touring in vaudeville under various names: Donna Hart, Helen Gardner, and Jill Cameron. For a time, she appeared in a number of revues and musicals on Broadway, including two editions of the *Garrick Gaieties*, *Shoot the Works*, and *Flying Colors*. (In *Shoot the Works*, produced by columnist Heywood Broun, Coca had a song written especially for her by George Gershwin. Two days before the show opened, a new songwriter named Ann Ronnell—she later wrote

cluded Henry Fonda.) Rehearsing in a chilly theater, Coca borrowed a camel's hair coat owned by Charles Walters, later an MGM director (*Easter Parade, Lili*). Since Walters was five foot eleven and weighed 155 pounds, Coca looked ludicrous—and knew it. She began to improvise a routine in which she parodied a strutting stripper, with the coat serving as a hilarious substitute for the usual spangled and abbreviated costume. Leonard Sillman saw it, liked it, and put it in the show, along with several other numbers, including her brilliant "furs" routine. Coca was hailed by the critics as a rising young comedienne. The revue, however, had only a modest run of 149 performances.

For the next few years, Coca appeared in Broadway revues (including another edition of *New Faces*) and toured with stock companies. In the summer of 1939, she joined Max Liebman's troupe at Tamiment, along with a bright young comedian named Danny Kaye. That fall the troupe braved Broadway with *The Straw Hat Revue*, which ran through early December.

Coca continued to tour with stock companies for some years, appearing occasionally in a short-lived revue on Broadway (*All in Fun*, 1940; *Concert Varieties*, 1945). She was also a popular attraction in smart supper clubs, where her deft pantomime and satirical humor were well received. In 1948, while touring in a road company of Anita Loos' *Happy Birthday*, Coca was asked by her former mentor Max Liebman to join the company of his first venture into television, the "Admiral Broadway Revue." Here, she began her association with Sid Caesar, which led the following year to "Your Show of Shows."

At the end of the run of "Your Show of Shows," Coca recalled how she began working with Caesar:

I remember how it happened. Max was looking around for sketches, and I suggested a routine called "Better Go Now,"

"Who's Afraid of the Big Bad Wolf?"—collared Broun and persuaded him to substitute her song for Gershwin's, arguing that he should be encouraging *new* talent.)

Her first real break came with the revue *New Faces*, produced by Leonard Sillman, with whom she had had a dancing act in vaudeville. (The new faces in-

Imogene Coca rehearsing with choreographer James Starbuck.

which I used to do in the theater with my husband. I was hoping that Max would let me do the sketch on television with my husband, but he suggested Sid instead. It was one of those going-to-the-movies pantomime things and the reaction to our performance was wonderful. It went over so well that when Sid and I went with Max into "Show of Shows," we continued doing pantomime numbers, and before we knew what was happening, we had become a team.*

On "Your Show of Shows," in tandem with Caesar or alone onstage, Coca was

* New York *World-Telegram*, March 9, 1954.

Imogene Coca and James Starbuck in "The Doll Song."

able to draw on her many years of experience in every phase of the entertainment field. Max Liebman has described the special talent she brought to the program:

"Of all the people who worked on 'Your Show of Shows,' Coca was the most theater-oriented. She brought a very versatile set of tools to a very demanding medium. She was the most disciplined performer of all the people I had—the discipline really arising out of her experience in the theater, where it is so important. She had a very deep affection for the theater and for the world of performing. She's a gifted dancer and also a gifted singer in her way —she's not a great vocalist except that she can do a coloratura as well as Lily Pons

used to do. She's a great singer in the way Fred Astaire is a great singer."

In his *Life* article, Ernest Havemann also wrote about Coca's singing ability:

Her voice is really an excellent one, although slight, and she can hit with perfect pitch every note from low F in the basso's range to the F above high C, something that very few opera singers can manage. Yet she chooses to make her torch songs sound like the flirtations of a playful lady elephant, and she turns a Wagner aria into a nightmare of desperate concentration, quivering glissandos, and narrow escapes from total disaster.

Apart from her performing talents, Max Liebman has commented on Coca's

Imogene Coca, James Starbuck, and company doing a hoedown.

Imogene Coca and sailors in "We Saw the Sea."

lovability: "Coca has the touch of greatness that can evoke tremendous sympathy from an audience. In television, you have to have some quality that makes the audience love you. This isn't true in pictures, nor in any other performing area. In television, though, if the people don't love you, you're through. You never get started if they don't love you."

And love her they did on "Your Show of Shows." Her sublime sense of the ridiculous, her palpable delight in entertaining the audience despite her inner fright, her ability to perform the broadest slapstick with an artist's delicacy, endeared her to television viewers.

She was, of course, the perfect foil for Sid Caesar. But as a solo performer, or partnered with choreographer-dancer James Starbuck, she could display her full range of talents. Drawing on her background in the theater, she was the consummate entertainer, ready to portray everything from a hillbilly ("Fatback, Louisiana") to a Hindu dancer ("Temple Bells"). As the tireless vaudevillian,

eager to please the people out front, she performed with infectious enthusiasm for a lost theater art. The songs were from the familiar repertoire—"I've Got a Lovely Bunch of Cocoanuts," "Glow Worm," "Way Down Yonder in New Orleans"—but she brushed them all with her warmth and charm. She had a special affection for the rollicking song-and-dance man of the English music halls, and in such songs as "Lovely Weather for Ducks," "A Paper Full of Fish and Chips," and "Ever So Slightly Late" (as a man-on-the-town trying to get by a sleeping wife), she was particularly ingratiating:

> There'll be such strife
> If you fumble and wake the wife
> When you're rolling home
> Ever so slightly late.

In the tradition of the theater she had known and loved for years, Coca was also adept at leading the company in performing musical numbers out of a vanished era, from the turn of the century to the twenties. On the very first show,

Imogene Coca and the ballet company in "Temple Bells."

Imogene Coca and the chorus in "Harrigan."

she offered her version of musical star Lillian Russell, here called "Lillian Bustle." As she toasts her many suitors, Platinum Pete gives her something different, something useful: a diamond-studded corset. This exchange follows:

PETE: *The bones are genuine U.S. steel.*
COCA: *Why, Pete, I can hardly contain myself.*
PETE: *That's why I got you the corset.*

Whereupon Lillian and her suitors burst into song. On other occasions, Coca carried on as a bubbly twenties flapper named Babs, guided the company of singers and dancers through "Everybody Step," and performed a spirited rendition of "Harrigan," dressed in tails and backed by an equally natty chorus line. On one program, in a number from a 1910 musical comedy, she offered instructions for expressing one's emotions delicately:

> *Ev'ry little movement*
> *Has a meaning all its own.*
> *Ev'ry thought and feeling*
> *By some posture can be shown.*

Most fans of "Your Show of Shows" remember Coca cavorting through a performance of a 1918 dance craze called the "Tickle Toe." At a party in a Newport mansion in honor of the yachting season, Coca, as the sweetheart of the social set, tells the enthralled partygoers about the dance:

COCA: *Just got in from gay New York.*
> *They've replaced the Castle Walk.*
> *On the stage I saw a sassy lassie*
> *With a classy chassis on a spree.*
> *And the dance she did that night*
> *Was so cute and gay and bright.*
> *Not the type of thing for*
>> *Mary Garden*
> *It was very hard on toe and knee.*
CHORUS: *And its name?*
COCA: *Wouldn't you know! Tickle Toe!*
CHORUS: *Tickle Toe!*
COCA: *Tickle Toe.*
> *Ev'rybody ought to know*
> *How to do the Tickle Toe.*
> *With its movement so inviting*
> *Sort of cute and so exciting.*
> *Tickle ickle Tickle Toe.*

Also in a nostalgic vein, Coca, in one sketch, played an eager trombonist of the twenties who tries to substitute for a

---

* The number appeared in a 1976 revival of the twenties musical *Going Up*.

Imogene Coca as a substitute trombone in a jazz band.

missing player in a jazz band. (The missing man is "Buzz" Hannegan, the best trombone man in the business, and, as the manager says, "without him the combo's like a Stutz Bearcat without gas.") After some sour notes and a few attempts to walk away from the scene, Coca finally joins them in a "hot" number.

Coca, of course, was a pixilated delight recalling the musical modes of another era. But it was when she could apply her sly, slightly wicked, wonderfully observant satirical sense to a timeless solo number that she was at her most triumphant. Throughout "Your Show of Shows," and earlier, on the "Admiral Broadway Revue," her versions of smirking, sexy, and seductive vamps lightly mocked every self-styled chanteuse whose throaty monotones had put audiences to sleep. On one occasion, she

Imogene Coca trying to ignite James Starbuck with a torch song.

was a wily wanton taunting Jack Russell with her "Red Silk Stockings and Green Perfume." On another, she was nightclub singer Lamarr Laroche, intoning a woe-laden ballad as she's hotly pursued by a millionaire, a gangster, a band leader, and a waiter, all of whom threaten to kill her and themselves if she refuses to go off with them. "I'm yours," she sings to each of them. "Only yours. Exclusively yours. No one else's . . . but yours!" (Illogically, she adds: "Because you are mine, this makes us ours!") Each lover gets the same reproach: "You took my lips and my arms. You took my heart and my head. I am a slave to you. I wish I were dead!" In yet another number, wrapped in a slinky dress, she urged her lover, James Starbuck, to "Get Out of Town." In each case, as she sang her heart out, the throbbing passion in her voice would barely conceal the underlying satirical message: how foolish to be expending so much energy and emotion on romantic entanglements.

On several programs, Coca rendered an impression of eternal seductress Marlene Dietrich in her famous role of Lola-Lola in *The Blue Angel*. One was a full-scale version of the movie, with Caesar as the desperately smitten professor. On an earlier program, Coca, in the Lola-Lola getup, intoned a song about her doomed love for a fickle American. With her frizzy blond hair, her abbreviated costume exposing shapely legs, and her whiskey baritone, the young Dietrich had always been a ripe subject for parody, and Coca—like Carol Channing years later—gave her full due. Straddling a chair, her face a morose mask, Coca sang Mel Tolkin's ballad about "Mon Amour Americaine":

> Mon amour Americaine . . .
> He is so . . . what you call . . .
>   well-heeled.
> He left me with the Marshall Plan.
> He went to work for Marshall Field.

Coca's ultimate parody of sexiness was

her celebrated version of a stripper (or should one say "takeoff" of a stripper?), the number she had performed two decades earlier in *New Faces* and also on the Admiral show. Here she moved gleefully through all the traditional motions of the ecdysiast, never once noticing or caring that she (1) is as sexy as a rumpled dishrag and (2) is wearing an ankle-length shabby topcoat. She comes on-stage in her coat and, grinning broadly at the audience, removes two barrettes from her hair. Following a brief demented dance about the stage, she raises the hem of her coat, to permit an intimate view of absolutely nothing. She brushes her hair with abandon, titters behind her hand, then begins some truly inspired business with her belt. She plays with the belt, her face expressing what she clearly regards as rampant seductiveness. She then removes the belt and prances about the stage, stripper style. (At one point, she turns her back to the audience and waves the belt back and forth across her jiggling posterior.)

The tempo increases: she looks down the front of her coat and grins broadly and happily at what she sees, then walks to the rear of the stage and boldly pulls open her coat—but with her back to the audience! In another uproarious send-up of the stripper's strut, she proudly vamps across the stage, like Gypsy Rose Lee on one of her best days. Finally, she moves behind the curtain, sticks her head out, grins, and drops the gamy coat. A fanfare, and this unlikely stripper leaps onto the stage—wearing another coat!*

In addition to her delicious spoofs of sexy ladies, Coca also aimed accurate

(though not terribly painful) barbs at the world of high fashion. She delighted in lightly mocking their pretensions and absurdities. She was the definitive haughty, self-important fashion model, but as in the case of her merry stripper, she fails to notice that her image is at grotesque odds with her delusions of grandeur. In Irvin Graham's "Model Song," she sings:

Who's the most beautiful model
   in the world?
The model of the model agency?
Who's the most beautiful model in
   the world?
ME!!
Have you noticed those hands so
   divine?
Those hands are mine.
Those grand little hands are mine!

Entranced with her own chic and beauty, Coca then proceeds to model a group of hats for the new season. The judges have apparently elected her "Miss Hat Face of 1950." (A loser mumbles a remark, and Coca asks suspiciously: "Did she say *Rat* Face?") In succession, she models, among others, the Opera Hat, which sports a pair of opera glasses perched on its top; the Holiday Hangover Hat, with its own handy champagne glass; and the Patriotic Hat, ablaze with sparkling firecrackers. ("Are you looking for something appropriate to wear on the glorious Fourth? Here's a sparkling little item. Of course, my friends object because every time I wear it, I blow my top!") She also models her Spring Garden Hat, which has a surprise extra: the flowers on the hat actually bloom. "It kinda grows on you, doesn't it," Coca remarks.

In one of her most famous numbers, Coca models fur coats that look as if they had not only seen better days but may have never had a *good* one. Coca, of course, is convinced that each fur is a thing of beauty:

Isn't this an attractive number? It's good,

* NBC's Department of Continuity Acceptance objected to the very *idea* of a striptease on television, but they finally saw the light of day. Max Liebman recalls that members of the department would attend the Friday run-through to see that nothing censorable took place. But the program was such a success from the beginning that Liebman was placed in an autonomous position. "They never wanted to see anything or pass on anything," he says.

Imogene Coca's striptease.

you know, for practically every occasion. It's so basic. And so black. Aren't the skins simply divine? They're so beautifully matched.

She models another "magnificent" skin: "Such depth and beauty. I wish you could feel it. Can't you just see yourself walking down Park Avenue? [The coat begins to shed profusely.] Oh, well, let's face it. Nothing's very durable these days." She is agog with admiration for the rattiest of the furs:

In my opinion, mind you, this is only my opinion . . . I certainly don't want to force it on you . . . you know what I admire about this? It's the sheer stark simplicity of it. . . . we're naming this Death of an Eager Beaver. . . .

With unassailable logic, Coca concludes her modeling session:

So why ever look like a witch?
Wrap her in beautiful silver blue
*   muskrat*
And you'll find
That a pretty girl
Is just like a pretty girl.

In one of her finest monologues, Coca plays a fashion plate who has been judged the best-dressed woman of the year. (She proclaims brazenly: "Everywhere I go, people stop and stare at me!") With unswerving confidence, the lady models her basic outfit, a tacky conglomerate of mismatched items. "Accessories," she points out, "make the costume," as she models her new-style shoes. "Most open-toed shoes only display one toe, but the smart open-toed shoe goes all the way." (We see a shot of a shoe unabashedly displaying all of Coca's toes.) She moves next to "the question of dresses":

According to the dictates of Paris, the latest thing in skirts is a slit. Some have

a slit in the back, some have a slit on the side. You will notice that I have forty-nine slits, one for each state and one for Alaska. . . .

She carries an outsize bag ("lovely but also functional"), lined with asbestos ("so clever if you happen to carry loose matches with you, as so many women do"). A huge makeup box is included "to refresh myself during the day," and for an extra supply of all-important perfume, that "faint aura that gives you a sense of mystery," she has stashed a seltzer bottle. The "final touch that tops off everything, that lovely little piece of feminine frippery that has come back in style," turns out to be a thoroughly tattered umbrella. Her advice? "My advice to the ladies is if you want to be well dressed, wear clothes!" She goes off bellowing her theme song:

Fashion! Fashion!
Fashion's a passion with me!

Since gentle satire was the keynote of her television persona on "Your Show of Shows," Coca, as a trained dancer, could easily extend this satire into the rarefied world of ballet. With Max Liebman's devotion to ballet as an impetus, and with the brilliant choreography and seasoned dancing ability of James Starbuck as firm support, Coca was able to shine in a series of self-contained ballet numbers (such as ballet versions of "Tom Sawyer" or "Pocahontas"), or in classical ballet excerpts that were both beautiful and uproariously funny. Starbuck, who was responsible for the program's musical production numbers ("Anything that moves is Jimmy's responsibility," Max Liebman would say), has this comment on Coca's dancing: "As a dancer, she'd try anything and she could *do* anything. I knew she'd been in vaudeville when she was young. We would have such good laughs when we did the ballets because we were always trying to do them as 'legit' as possible."

This was the central concept: to perform the ballets authentically—and then add the requisite touch of comedy. Starbuck would take a well-known ballet and use its actual framework, just as it would be performed at the Ballet Russe de Monte Carlo, where he had worked. He would direct Coca and the company of dancers in the same fashion as he would any of the celebrated dancers who appeared on the program. Then, using the formalized steps of the ballet, he would play against them, introducing a comedy element. Starbuck notes that Coca was continuously fretting about the ballet numbers. "I'll never be Markova," she would moan.

The results were splendid, and Coca's numbers with Starbuck, performing scenes from *Sleeping Beauty, Les Sylphides, Giselle, Afternoon of a Faun,* and many other well-known ballets, are among the most fondly remembered of "Your Show of Shows." In *Sleeping Beauty,* for example, Starbuck used the same formations, the same steps as in the original ballet. Except that he and Coca blithely took the sleeping princess into the realm of inspired visual comedy.

We come upon Princess Imogene asleep with her ladies- and gentlemen-in-waiting. The Prince (Starbuck) enters, wakes them all except Coca, and proceeds to dance with them. He bends to kiss Coca, and then, in a sublimely funny moment, she opens one large, suspicious eye. He kisses her again, but she continues to sleep. Finally he gives her a firm push, and she comes awake—only to sleepwalk right back into her comfortable bed. He stirs her awake again, and they dance, with Coca yawning as they go through the positions. Again she goes back to bed, and again he rouses her. They dance, and Coca also dances with her men-in-waiting, taking pleasure in making each of them spin in place at her command. She then gets lifted by each man, only to be left dangling absurdly from one of the pillars. The men give her bouquets (she playfully bops one of them on the head with the flowers), and now it is the men's turn to spin Coca around in place, each taking a turn in whirling her about. She dances once again with the Prince—at one point she expresses annoyance at not being able to disengage his hand—then goes blissfully back to sleep.

As in all the ballet sequences, Coca's dancing proficiency and comic genius combine with unforgettable results. And yet, Starbuck points out, Coca was never fully satisfied. She would have "ten million fits each time," he says. "She always believed she could never do as well as she did the last time."

One of the most delightful and intricate ballet sequences was the Pas de Deux from *Les Sylphides*, in which two bored ballet dancers (Coca and Starbuck) go through the motions while discussing mundane matters:

COCA: *I went to Nora's party last night.*
STARBUCK: *How was it? Who was there?*
COCA: *Nobody who was anybody. . . . Nora*

introduced me to a man. A toothpick manufacturer. . . . Five minutes after we were introduced, he asked me up to his place to listen to symphony records. I told him!*
STARBUCK: *What did you say?*
COCA: *I said: "Listen Mr. Ludlow, don't go getting any ideas just because I'm in the ballet."*
STARBUCK: *So what did he say?*
COCA: *He said: "I only want to show you my collection of records."*
STARBUCK: *So what did you say?*
COCA: *I said: "Listen, if you were Ezio Pinza and you wanted to give me a private concert, I wouldn't go after only knowing you for five minutes!"*
STARBUCK: *So what did he say?*
COCA: *He said: "All right, don't go. See if I care."*
STARBUCK: *So what happened?*
COCA: *He has a very nice collection of records.*

Coca had first performed several of her ballet numbers at Tamiment, and one of

Imogene Coca as a lovable tramp and James Starbuck as a dancing scarecrow.

Imogene Coca and James Starbuck in a comic ballet.

the most widely applauded had been her very special version of *Swan Lake*. As the hapless heroine who is transformed by a sorcerer into a swan, she achieved a remarkable feat: to the Tchaikovsky music, against an authentic setting, wearing (like the chorus members) an impeccably correct costume, she drew on all her formidable comic resources to tilt the ballet in the direction of laughter. She sheds her swan's feathers all over the stage, tries to shake away an annoying kink in her neck, finds herself unable to rise from one position, becomes dizzy from too much twirling, and is left dangling clumsily on a wire over the heads of the other dancers. Her inventiveness is boundless: at one point she performs a fast, brief, eccentric dance about the stage in which she resembles a demented duck rather than a graceful swan. At another, to lure James Starbuck, she uses her swan's wings in the manner made famous by Sally Rand. The lovely music soars, but so does Coca in her own inimitable way.

Certainly one of the funniest of the ballet sequences was Coca's version of *Scheherazade*, a lavishly staged send-up of every "exotic" musical number ever performed in movie "Easterns" or on the giant stage of New York's Radio City Music Hall. As the haughty princess with an insatiable fondness for bananas, Coca was a riotous cartoon version of Maria Montez and Yvonne De Carlo in their "Arabian Nights" days.

The ballet begins with a gruff and bearded Shah (James Starbuck) surrounded by the girls of his harem. Indifferent to their brief dance (to Rimsky-Korsakov's music), he dismisses them all, the better to savor the delights of the irresistible Scheherazade. Enter Coca as Scheherazade, carried aloft by the Shah's men and casually munching a banana. (As usual, Coca's rendition of sultry sexiness is magnificent.) The Shah offers her jewels and his undivided attention, and when she shows no signs of responding, he threatens her with a scimitar. It's be faithful or beheaded, he warns her. When he leaves, Coca makes a very unprincesslike gesture of rude dismissal.

With nothing much else to do, Scheherazade dances with the Shah's men. They whirl around her as she shrugs with boredom; they lift her up in a most "klutzy" fashion, and she is still disinterested. Her only pleasure comes from

making them leap up and down in their places, or having them crouch as she walks barefooted across their backs. Finally, she resigns herself to eating another banana.

The Shah returns, furious and out for blood. She tries to tiptoe away but he drags her back. With his scimitar at the very tip of her nose, he threatens to kill her on the spot. They grapple and she manages to break free by tickling him.

Now Scheherazade tries her unfailing ploy: seduction. Coyly waving her banana peel in his face, grinning in Coca-esque fashion, she lures him to her, then rejects him. Dancing around him, she manages to get his knife. When he offers her jewels again, she pulls the knife and holds him at bay. Summoning his men, she has them carry her out as triumphantly as she had entered. As she leaves, she swipes at a banana that just happens to be hanging from a chandelier and proceeds to peel it. Her face registers the cruel smugness of a woman whose sexual wiles have conquered danger. It is also the face of a most gifted dancing comedienne.

The ballet world was not the only target of Coca's affectionate mockery. At times, she would also poke fun at the amusing excesses of grand opera. In one of the first shows, she was a great opera star recalling when she sang the leading role in that beautiful Wagnerian opus *Du Bist Mein Herzen's Liebe in the Sheida of the Old Apple Tree*. On another program, she was uproarious as the disruptive member of a quartet performing in *Rigoletto*. As a local citizen substituting for a missing singer in a traveling opera company, Coca appeared onstage with Bill Hayes, Jack Russell, and Adrianna Knowles, grinning happily at her big chance to attract attention.

She begins by insisting on holding a note much too long, but the more pressing problem is that she clearly has a crush on tenor Hayes. As the aria progresses, she leers at him, sidles up to him, and

The quartet from Rigoletto: *Adrianna Knowles, Bill Hayes, Imogene Coca, and Jack Russell.*

even stands in front of him. She becomes irritated when he turns his attentions to Adrianna Knowles, tries to catch his eye, and ends up tickling him furiously as he tries to sing. When Jack Russell tries to be ardent in the prescribed manner, she rejects him and confronts Knowles with a baleful eye. All to no avail: Hayes succeeds in avoiding her, and try as she might, she ends up in Russell's waiting arms. The scene is beautifully carried out by Coca, but what makes it remarkable is that the aria is performed creditably by the four singers. There is no attempt to burlesque the number with dreadful voices, and even the slapstick is handled with finesse.

On another program, Coca was the central figure in the famous aria performed by the sextette in *Lucia di Lammermoor*. Here the premise was that the tenor next to Coca had recently eaten garlic, and her desperate attempt to sing the aria while avoiding his garlic fumes was the basis for the comedy. She clings to another singer but cannot escape the amorous attentions of the garlic-breathing tenor. She fans herself, raises her eyes to the heavens for divine intervention, and, at one point, faces the camera with a

look of open-mouthed horror. As the aria rings forth (again, faithful in all respects to Donizetti), she weaves her way through the other singers but he pursues her tirelessly. Finally, she staggers and, with the last notes of the aria, sinks prostrate on the floor.

Yet of all the guises in which Coca appeared on "Your Show of Shows," none was as cherished or as unforgettable as her Tramp. Brought back many times over the run of the program, her Tramp had the sweetness, the hopefulness, and the plaintiveness of Chaplin's immortal creation, but Coca, of course, embellished the character with her singing and dancing skills. (Chaplin's movements were often balletic, and W. C. Fields was said to have stormed out of a showing of one of Chaplin's films, bellowing "Goddamned ballet dancer!")

The highlight of many a Saturday night program was the sight of Coca in her tramp costume, wistfully singing in her quavering voice about her optimistic frame of mind: "Life Is Just a Bowl of

Tramp with trombone.

Cherries," "I'm Just a Dreamer with a Penny," "I Haven't Time to Be a Millionaire," "Give Me the Simple Life," and others. In "A Nickel's Worth of Sunshine," she found a discarded tutu near a ballet theater and, wearing it over her tramp costume, she performed an enchanting dance. In "The Whistling Kettle and the Dancing Cat," she was joined by two Bil Baird puppets in a number that had kettle, cat, and Coca joining in a song and dance that would surely earn smiles from a stone. In "The Magic Lamp," the Tramp rubbed an old kerosene lamp and was transformed into an unlikely Arabian princess, who at one point does a marvelous send-up of the slinky dance usually expected of Arabian princesses. Occasionally, Coca was partnered in her tramp numbers with James Starbuck, who in various guises—a janitor, a store window dummy, a scarecrow—would be coaxed by Coca into sharing the joyful spirit of her song and dance.

One of the best remembered of Coca's tramp numbers was performed to the standard tune "Wrap Your Troubles in Dreams." (It was reprised with stunning poignancy on the final show.) Here she begins by singing to a very proper doorman (Starbuck) of a posh apartment house. She faces the camera as it moves in for a closeup, and her expression is clearly suspended between laughter and tears. She teases the doorman into relaxing and dancing with her, and soon they are sprinting about the street and enjoying themselves immensely. The doorman becomes irritated when they exchange hats by mistake, and he blows his whistle. A street cleaner enters, pushing a garbage cart. Coca perches on it and reprises the song, now closer to tears. She rides off the stage on the cart, leaving behind the very proper doorman, and an audience that never forgot the touching gift she had bestowed upon them.

In his New York *Herald-Tribune* column on September 26, 1952, John Crosby commented on this number:

She hadn't much to work with. She was dressed as a tramp and was singing the song to a rather stuffy doorman. She has that rare facility of singing a song as if she not only understood the words but meant every word of it. The number ended with a little dance which was just great; no smaller word would apply. Then the doorman blew his whistle; a street cleaner came up with his little cart and Miss Coca made a perfectly wonderful exit perched on the cart.

It was a very sweet, heart-warming number with just an overtone of mockery to keep it from getting too sticky. And it was the sort of thing that sticks to your ribs, a number that you may recall with pleasure long after it's over. How many song-and-dance numbers can you recall ten minutes after they're finished?

Plaintive tramp or wicked wanton, leering stripper or balmy ballerina, Imogene Coca was a consummate artist on "Your Show of Shows." Like Sid Caesar, she was able to project a foolish and endearing humanity, a sense of joy in the absurd behavior of people as they coped (or tried to cope) with life. Shorn of this humanity, some of her solo performances could have become overly sweet. But in every comic characterization she assumed, she wore her credentials as a recognizable person, fallible and funny.

6

Caesar and Coca- Together!

If in her solo performances Coca was a blessing we could all share, when she joined with Sid Caesar we were twice blessed. He was a sturdily built, handsome man of simple needs and appetites, blustering and blundering his way through an insurmountable number of grievances. A man traveling uneasily and suspiciously down life's highway and finding detours, roadblocks, and wrong directions. She was a petite, energetic, infinitely adorable woman whose face could register an extraordinary variety of moods and attitudes, from unbridled lust to towering rage. A woman who, on one hand, was in relentless pursuit of culture and the "finer things," and on the other, thumbed her nose at them with raffish glee. These are the personae developed and nurtured by Sid Caesar and Imogene Coca on

"Your Show of Shows," and they could not have been more disparate.

Yet together on the small screen, they generated a rapport that was inimitable. In a series of sketches as television's most talented duo, they played off and with and against each other with a felicity that was a pleasure to watch. Nose to nose in a moment of confrontation as Doris and Charlie Hickenlooper, pantomiming a driving lesson or a ride on a roller coaster, or mouthing a series of deadly accurate platitudes on a variety of subjects, they made the routine television comedy of the day seem cruder and more antiquated than it already was. Max Liebman said it best in 1951: "Here are two comedians who are helping each other instead of competing for laughs. Its screwy; it's something that doesn't happen. Yet it is happening, and it works." Caesar agreed wholeheartedly and remarked: "The first time I met Imogene was at an NBC rehearsal hall. Max Liebman was getting the 'Admiral Broadway Revue' together and he introduced us to each other. I felt a certain chemistry between us immediately. Right away, I called her 'Immie' and that's all I ever called her.'" Today, so many years later, Caesar feels the same way: "The chemistry was magical."

Howard Morris, who supported them brilliantly in many sketches, said of this rapport: "Sid would have the courage to stay with something big enough and long enough to make it work just by repetition, by dunning away at it. By tapping away at the rock, you eventually reach water. He's not very good at words—he's developed a way of communicating with a mass of words. Coca was a little more careful with words. Her gentle delicacy played against his hugeness—and they would be clanging together against each other."

One of the formulas that evolved for their joint appearances on the program had been developed in the years at Tamiment. This was the "cliché" sketch, in

which Caesar and Coca would meet for the first time, strangers sharing a particular moment or situation. All they really had in common was a boundless ability to express every conceivable cliché on the topic at hand, and an inexhaustible penchant for telling hilariously pointless stories. In these sketches, they were every man and woman with an unwavering (and unjustified) belief in the absolute *rightness* of his or her attitude.

On one occasion, they meet in a divorce court where mutual friends are untying the knot. They contemplate the factors that caused the rift:

COCA: *Well, I just can't understand it. I expected their marriage to go on forever. They had so much in common, you know.*

CAESAR: *That's right. The same interests. They liked the same things.*

COCA: *He liked baseball.*

CAESAR: *And so did she.*

COCA: *He liked to collect stamps.*

CAESAR: *And so did she.*

COCA: *He liked to go out with the boys at night and drink and play poker and smoke cigars.*

CAESAR: *And so did she.*

They talk about the role played by the mysterious "third party," the inevitable "other woman":

COCA: *That woman had no right to come between them.*

CAESAR: *Well, what are you gonna do? I guess the other woman was more important than his wife.*

COCA: *She certainly alienated his affections. At first it was just once or twice a week, he'd come home later. But she knew where he had been. Then finally it seems he just didn't even care to hide it anymore. It got to a point where he went there for dinner every single night. You can imagine how she felt. She finally faced him with it. She said: "What do you think I am, blind? I know what's been going on. You'll have to choose between us. It's either me or your mother."*

Coca tells Caesar about the morning that brought everything "to a head," when they knew the marriage was over:

COCA: *He came in to breakfast, didn't say good morning. Picked up the newspaper and buried himself in it without a glance at her. Then he took a drink of coffee and spit it out and said: "You call this coffee? This tastes miserable." And she said: "Is that so? Well, there's nothing wrong with my coffee. That happens to be poison. I make very good coffee."*

CAESAR: *Well, I don't think it was the poison that bothered him. It was something that went much deeper . . . a knife.*

In these sketches, Caesar and Coca often appeared as parents meeting at the initiation of their respective children into one of life's early rituals. For example, when they register their children for school, they are pleased to discover that they went to the same school, and even had a teacher in common. (Each of these sketches would lead inevitably to a joint cry of "Isn't it a *small* world!"):

CAESAR: *In third grade, I had Miss Canterbury.*

COCA: *Why, isn't it a coincidence! So had I! What an angel she was!*

CAESAR: *She certainly knew how to handle children.*

COCA: *The sweetest disposition.* [They both laugh] *Remember the tricks we played on her.*

CAESAR: *Do I remember! I'll never forget how we threw spitballs right during class.*

COCA: *And how we used to walk out of class whenever we wanted to and came late to school.*

CAESAR: *And then we'd draw her face on the blackboard.*

COCA: *And she took it all with a smile.*

CAESAR: *Nothing bothered her.* [Pause] *She went crazy.*

They discuss the rearing of children with a sagacity gleaned from reading every "advice" column in the newspaper:

COCA: *You know, raising children is such a problem.*

CAESAR: *I certainly agree with you!*

COCA: *I mean even with all the psychology books.*

CAESAR: *In fact, they only confuse you. Some say, be kind to them. Some say, be firm. Some say, use discipline, some say, let them have their own way.*

COCA: *Well, I think that these books generalize too much. The way I look at it, each child is an individual problem.*

CAESAR: *There are no two children alike.*

COCA: *I mean, two children can be raised in the same environment—*

CAESAR: *—and get the same opportunities,*

the same background, be treated the same way, and one grows up to be a crook, and the other a murderer.

COCA: *Like father—*

CAESAR: *—like son.*

Naturally, there are small problems to contend with, but nothing serious. Perhaps a child with an odd reaction to food:

CAESAR: *You know, my big problem with my child is to get it to eat. I mean mealtime is very trying. I have to put on a whole show for my girl, tell stories, about the big lion and the little lion, and to taste the food so the child doesn't think* it's poison. I simply can't get that child to eat!

COCA: *Well, my son just puts it away . . . just puts it away!*

CAESAR: *Is that right?*

COCA: *Doesn't eat a thing. Just puts it away. Children must have nourishment.*

CAESAR: *Certainly. Because from little acorns—*

CAESAR AND COCA: *—big oaks grow.*

As the "little acorns" grow, they require a little diversion from their grueling routine, and so our parents meet again when they send the children off to sum-

Sid Caesar and Imogene Coca rehearsing the pantomime "Summer Resort."

Imogene Coca and Sid Caesar in a cliché sketch: registering their children for school.

mer camp. Caesar describes last year's camp to an interested Coca, and, incidentally, demonstrates a favorite gambit of the writers—the expected ending that gets turned on its head, dissolving a surprised audience in laughter:

CAESAR: *You know, last year I sent my boy to a Western camp. Real Wild West stuff, you know. Taught them how to ride horses and use a lasso. They walked around in Hopalong Cassidy hats, and Hopalong Cassidy guns. And you know who came to visit them around rodeo time, in person . . . Gloria Swanson! She wore a Hopalong Cassidy suit.*

He also explains how his son learned the surest way to survive in a juvenile jungle:

The best thing is the things the children learn at camp and the way they get built up physically. For instance, my little boy used to be a very weak, scrawny kid. No muscles, thin as a rail, afraid of other kids. They used to gang up on him and beat him up. Well, after he came back from camp, they didn't bother him anymore. He came back a changed person. As soon as he learned how to throw that knife, they left him alone. What a wonderful camp!

He adds by way of explanation: "It was a knife-throwing camp."

Sid also answers the question every parent must have asked himself at one time: Do I *want* a disciplined child? He sends his son to Camp Sitstraight, where the boy learns to be a perfect gentleman, speaking only when spoken to, rising when a lady enters the room, addressing his father politely. Sid's reaction: "At home he'd keep saying: 'Dad, may I leave the table?' 'Dad, may I speak to Mater?' ...Dad this, Dad that...I wanted to smash his face!'"

One of the funniest encounters comes at the ceremonies for the public school graduation of their children. His son and her daughter are graduating, and it's a time for rejoicing, except for the fact that Mother Coca's girl sounds slightly peculiar:

COCA: *There's my daughter ... fourth from the right.*
CAESAR: *Oh, I see her. The redhead with the plunging neckline and the high heels.*
COCA: *It's a stage she's going through. In a couple of weeks, she'll be back to her natural brown hair. Where's your son?*
CAESAR: *He's the one standing right next to your daughter with his mouth open.*

Apparently, Coca's daughter is mature in other ways as well:

COCA: *Nowadays, they teach children much more practical things, I'm happy to say. For instance, my daughter had a course in domestic science, and she really learned how to cook. She's very good at it. In fact, on weekends, she works as a short order cook in Joe's Diner.*

In the polite world of clichés, nobody is flappable. "Oh, yes," Caesar responds. "I've eaten there. The food is very good."

At one point, Caesar and Coca discuss a "wonderful" teacher, Miss Wilson:

COCA: *She's the head of Arts and Crafts. She did the decorations. Isn't it clever the way she blended in the school colors? I*
think the school colors are really appropriate, don't you? They give the feeling of children at play.*
CAESAR: *Yes. Black and blue. I think that's a wonderful portrait of Ulysses S. Grant with his heavy eyebrows, his strong, sharp nose, and his thick beard.*
COCA: *That's not Ulysses S. Grant. That's Miss Wilson.*
CAESAR: *I guess in the excitement she forgot to shave.*

Away from the educational scene, Caesar and Coca are still addicted to the hackneyed phrase, still inclined to relate anecdotes that change points in midstream or are miracles of long-winded pointlessness. Here they are, trotting out every cherished belief about the virtues of dogs, and then exploding them neatly:

CAESAR: *I like a playful dog. I once had a Great Dane. They're so playful and affectionate, you know. Whenever he'd see me, he'd jump up and knock me down, tear my clothes, and drag me all over the living room floor ...I was afraid to go home.*
COCA: *Dogs are really faithful. We had a neighbor of ours who treated his dog miserably ... never fed him on time. Well, one day he just up and left. That dog didn't leave that front porch. He was faithful. Well, about two years later, the master returned. The dog just stood there, watching his master come down the path and onto the porch.*
CAESAR: *And then what happened?*
COCA: *[Barest pause] Ripped him to pieces.*
CAESAR: *And they're protective. I had a neighbor whose dog was certainly protective. He'd really guard that house. Nobody could get within a hundred feet of that place. I'll never forget the night when we were standing there and watching the house burn down. ...*

Another time, they meet at a dentist's office, fully prepared to face the ordeal, and to exchange "advanced" ideas on dental care and treatment:

COCA: *I believe in getting a cavity filled right away. An ounce of prevention . . . you know, is the best cure.*

CAESAR: *Oh, yes. Sometimes two ounces. Just hold it next to the tooth. Takes the pain right away.*

COCA: *Well, I have a lot of trouble with my teeth, you know. And there's a reason for it. Lack of calcium.*

CAESAR: *Oh, that'll do it every time!*

COCA: *I just don't have enough calcium in my system. Lots of people don't, you know. There are some people who say it has to do with the drinking water. For instance, there's a little town upstate that has the most amazing drinking water in the country! Some chemical in it that's very necessary for teeth. And would you believe it, there's not one person in that town who ever had a cavity! They all have perfect teeth! Of course they're all bald . . . but their teeth are perfect.*

Not to be outdone, Sid also has an anecdote to offer on the subject of teeth:

CAESAR: *I personally think a lot of people could save their teeth if they didn't indulge themselves, you know . . . eating sweets. I knew a case once of a woman who had the most beautiful set of teeth you ever saw. Pearls! But she loved to eat sweets. It drove her husband crazy. He used to say: "Alice, if you don't stop eating those sweets, you're going to lose your teeth!" But she wouldn't listen, and sure enough, two weeks later, all her front teeth were missing!*

COCA: *From eating sweets?*

CAESAR: *No. He knocked them out. She wouldn't listen, and it aggravated him. So he let her have it.*

Sid also expounds the theory that bad teeth can affect other parts of your body, give you a backache or even eyestrain. As an example, he tells about his brother who found he was limping. He went to his doctor, who diagnosed the trouble

Caesar and Coca cavorting in a tramp ballet.

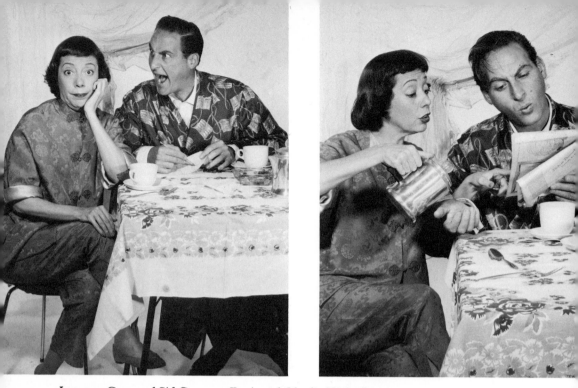

Imogene Coca and Sid Caesar as Doris and Charlie Hickenlooper.

as his teeth. Coca is mystified until Caesar explains:

CAESAR: *His teeth were causing the pain in his foot! His bridge had fallen into his shoe and the teeth were biting into his big toe!*

COCA: *Isn't that something!*

Coca tells Caesar about "the latest thing in painless dentistry." It seems that the injection is given right behind the ears.

CAESAR: *What good does it do back there?*

COCA: *It deadens the nerves in the ear, so you can't hear yourself screaming.*

On their trek down the long and venerable road of clichés, Caesar and Coca visit their doctors, attend a cocktail party and a wedding reception, compare literary notes in a book store, and meet in a courtroom. On one occasion, they pause to discuss the subject of superstition, as they wait in a tearoom for a gypsy to read their fortunes:

CAESAR: *Superstition is a vicious thing.*

Just to show you what superstition will do . . . we had a sweet little old lady in our town. Gray-haired, with spectacles, you know. A very nice old lady. Well, somebody started a rumor about her. They said she was a witch. They said when she walked past a garden, the flowers would wilt and die. They ran her out of town. I felt terrible about it. [Pause] Of course it did wonders for the flowers.

COCA: *Well, you know, we live in a house that's supposed to be haunted. It's perfectly ridiculous. Of course, I will admit that every night at the stroke of twelve—*

CAESAR: *—the witching hour—*

COCA: *—the witching hour. Every night, this creature appears, all in white, glides down the stairs, across the living room floor, right up to the bar, drinks half a quart of whiskey—glides back across the living room, up the stairs, and disappears.*

CAESAR: *Well, aren't you scared?*

COCA: *Oh no, it's my father. And besides, we water the whiskey. We have to humor* him, you know. He's getting along in years.

We'll leave our cliché experts on their Christmas shopping rounds as Caesar holds a conversation with Coca that reveals a few surprising sides to his hearty personality:

COCA: *You know, it's a funny thing about children. They really have no idea of the value of a gift. It doesn't really matter how expensive it is. You can buy them all kinds of magnificent toys and yet they'll have some little old raggedy doll that they've had and they form an attachment to it and no matter how many new presents they get, they'll go on dragging this little old toy around for years and years.*

CAESAR: *That's true. That's very true.* [He pulls a raggedy doll out of his pocket, kisses it, and puts it back] *Linda, Linda, Linda....*

At another point in the conversation, Sid comments on the frequent mixup of gifts at Christmastime:

CAESAR: *Christmas is so hectic. People sometimes mix up their gifts when they're wrapping them and send the wrong gift to the wrong person. Last year, you'll never believe what I got. Three pairs of the sheerest nylon stockings. But under the pants they don't show. I'll never get used to wearing a garter belt, though....*

A final observation before they go their separate ways:

COCA: *Sometimes it's very difficult to make up your mind. I have so much trouble deciding what to buy. I guess I'm not alone, though. Look at that woman over there. She can't decide whether to take the bracelet or the necklace. She keeps hesitating and hesitating. Oh, she took the necklace.*

CAESAR: *Yes, and look at that man beside her. He's hesitating, too. He doesn't know whether to arrest her now or when she gets out of the store.*

The Man and Woman of the cliché sketches were anonymous people confronting and assessing their experiences with a keen ear for the mundane. Doris and Charles Hickenlooper, on the other hand, were flesh-and-blood people, each snugly inhabiting a persona that varied little from sketch to sketch. This man and wife may have seldom indulged in the knockdown slapstick of Lucy and Desi, or the boisterous bickering of Ralph and Alice Kramden, but they were truer, more honestly observed, and funnier.*

Doris Hickenlooper, in the person of Imogene Coca, is a woman whose tiny frame conceals a large appetite for new experiences. A fiercely determined and relentless culture-vulture, social climber, and food snob, she is a basically grim creation made laughable and lovable through the genius of Coca. Confronted with a lumbering, loutish husband whose social graces and aspirations are non-existent, she reacts with varying degrees of exasperation and rage. She can complain bitterly to her mother over the telephone, raise her voice to a clamorous pitch, thrust her formidable jaw at her thick-skulled husband, or (most effectively) use words like whips to beat him into submission.

Example: Doris is engaged in spring cleaning and has just received a complaint from Charlie about the "good" things she's throwing out. Her words become a ferocious assault on his attitude:

COCA: *Why don't you face it? There are certain things that have just seen their day! You may have something around the house that once used to have a place here, but it outlived its usefulness. You don't really need it anymore, it just takes*

* Lucille Kallen has remarked that Max Liebman would receive letters from all over the country about the Hickenlooper sketches. One said: "You have no idea what a great service you are doing. You are showing us how silly we are when we behave that way. It's very true and very real."

up space . . . face the facts! To keep hold-ing onto it is nothing but sheer senti-mentality! Don't you think it's silly to hold on to something that at one time you have been madly in love with, but today has lost all its glamour, and is just a relic?

Caesar pauses for what seems like an eternity, looks her up and down, and replies quietly: "I guess I'm just a senti-mental fool!"

Charlie Hickenlooper, on the other hand, is a clumsy bear of a man, trying to cope with this tough little tigress—and getting nowhere. A strong and rough-hewn man, he can only react phys-ically to Doris's mental gymnastics, dis-torting his face to convey dismay, out-rage and fury, his entire person quivering as he is dragged once again into another strange and upsetting environment by his upwardly mobile wife. Charlie has simple wants: his supper, a comfortable chair, freedom from hassle, relative peace and quiet, and an occasional poker game with friends. What he gets is Doris, urging him to try new things, provoking him into fierce quarrels, or continually baffling him as she sets about changing their lives. At home, he would like to be king of his castle, but he is a king without subjects, only one rebel ready to knock the crown from his head. She is smaller than he is, but better armed.

For Doris, life is a continual search for the "finer things": elegant home furnishings, priceless antiques, glorious symphonic music—and exotic foods. Eat-ing may not be one of her passions, but finding new places to eat is one of her favorite pursuits—and so off she goes in many a sketch with a reluctant Charlie in tow. On one occasion, she takes him kicking and screaming to an East Indian restaurant where Carl Reiner, as the headwaiter, greets them effusively:

REINER: [Bowing] The ancient house of the Golden Lamb is your servant, O honored guests. May the grass grow tall for the goats of your father's father, and your children drink the wine of abun-dance that grows as the grapes on the vine of your mother's mother . . .

CAESAR: [Rising with clenched fist] I ought to belt you!

When Sid tries to cope with the ethnic dishes, at Coca's insistence, the result is uproarious:

CAESAR: What have you got to eat?

REINER: Klochmoloppi. We also have lich lock, slop lom, shtocklock, rishkosh, and flocklish.

CAESAR: Yuch!

REINER: We have yuch, too. Boiled or braised?

On another occasion, Doris drags a reluctant Charlie into a health food restaurant to experience the pleasures of "natural" food. As expected, he is not keen on the idea:

CAESAR: Doris, you know I don't like to experiment. Why start in with strange new things like health foods? I'm hungry. Let's go to Pepito's. We can get spiced snails in tabasco sauce, some hot tamales, and pepperone sausages with the mustard and pickles. After all, why take chances with your stomach? You don't know what you're getting here.

But Doris persists, and Charlie soon finds himself nibbling at a flower picked from the vase on the table, which turns out to be a "blossom of the palipoca plant, chock full of thangamese oxide." "It's wonderful for your ankles," says Doris. Charlie is not impressed: "The next time we eat out, we'll eat separately. I'll eat in Pepito's, you eat in the Botani-cal Gardens."

Undaunted, Doris scans the menu: "Vegetable protein derivative. Yeast ex-tract. Low sodium manganese salad. I can't make up my mind. Everything sounds so yum yummy." Waiter Carl Reiner tries to be helpful: "Why don't you try the Vitamin B1, B3, D, and H dinner for two?" Finally, to Charlie's disgust (brought to the ultimate degree by Caesar), Doris orders the homogenized bone meal, wheat germ, and a side order of glucose. Ever-helpful, Reiner explains that "glucose doesn't come with the wheat germ," but he could substitute "crotose."

COCA: *I don't care for crotose. Have you any pirotose?*

REINER: *Not on Fridays. How about serutose?*

Playfully, Charlie orders a broiled elm tree on toast, only to get a sober response from Reiner: "That is not on the menu, sir."

For Charlie, even a lobster house can become a hostile environment in which his digestive system will suffer permanent damage. He would rather go where he can get "a good meal—steak and potatoes"—but Doris is again determined to broaden his gastronomic horizons. "This is a *seafood* restaurant," she explains. "You can get things here that you never *tasted* before. I want you to try something *new* for a change." "I don't want to try something new. I'm hungry," surly Charlie replies.

COCA: *You know what the trouble is with you? [She's glad to tell him] You have no spirit of adventure! Didn't you ever try something new, strange, unusual, a little off the beaten path, something a little weird, something you thought you'd never have anything to do with.*

CAESAR: *[Looks at her] Once.*

He is finally induced to read the menu:

CAESAR: *Scrambled snails baked in scrod sauce. [Looks at her, reads again] Spare ribs of swordfish sautéed in seaweed, octopus toenails, smothered in fried minnows. [Gets up to go] Come on.*

Doris persists, and Charlie must finally face his first lobster. His reaction is to leap up in fright and cry: "They're alive!"

Reassured that the lobsters are alive to keep them fresh, he is asked to choose the one he'd like:

CAESAR: *You mean I have to choose which one you're going to kill? I have to pronounce the death sentence?*

COCA: *That's right.*

CAESAR: *How do they die?*

COCA: *They boil them in hot water until they turn pink.*

CAESAR: *[Looking at her] Doris, you're a hard woman. [Then he decides to choose, points with his finger] Eany meany miney moe—ow! [He grabs his finger away] Kill him!*

Even at home, Doris has a refined taste in food that baffles and discomfits poor Charlie. Rummaging through the refrigerator for a midnight snack, he finds—not "plenty of food," as Doris insists—but watercress, parsley, turnip greens, maraschino cherries, ketchup, mustard, salt, and pepper. "A meal fit for a king!" he cries. Finally, he discovers a piece of cheese.

CAESAR: *[Puzzled] What kind of cheese is this?*

COCA: *Limhoffer cheese.*

CAESAR: *It's supposed to be like this? Blue and green . . . with yellow fuzz on top of it, and a purple streak down the middle?*

COCA: *Certainly that's how it's supposed to be. It's very good. Try it. They make it purposely that way. They take a big lump of cheese and they leave it in a damp, musty cellar until it gets moldy.*

Needless to say, Charlie does not consume the cheese.

Of course Doris Hickenlooper's aspirations extend beyond gourmet dining. Inevitably, she must attend a concert in Symphony Hall to nourish her soul as well as her body. Unfortunately, the body that accompanies her to the concert belongs to that eternal vulgarian, Charlie. While Doris waxes enthusiastic, Charlie is bored and grouchy:

COCA: *Oh, look! In the second half of the program they're playing Tchaikovsky's Pathetic Symphony. Tchaikovsky had a very pathetic life, you know. When you hear his music, you actually feel all the pain and agony and torture and misery.*

CAESAR: *I got my own aggravation. I don't have to come here and listen to his torture.*

COCA: *You'll enjoy this. Look . . . the musicians are taking their places.* [Sound of orchestra tuning up]

CAESAR: [Listens for a while] *He must've had a miserable life.*

COCA: *They're just tuning up.*

In ceaseless pursuit of the rich life, Doris also longs to fill her home with "priceless possessions." She forces a highly dubious Charlie to attend an antiques auction, where she tells him: "Now that you got a raise, we ought to live up to our position in life. I want to have an elegant home. I want to be so proud of it that I won't be afraid to invite anybody." Charlie, of course, has other ideas on the subject. When Doris admires a chair as "Louie the 14th," he tells her scornfully: "I could get the same chair from Louie the Janitor. . . . He wouldn't even keep it in his cellar." When the auction begins, however, he finds himself deliriously caught up in the spirit of competition. (When Howie Morris, as another buyer, outbids him on an item he bid for during his delirium, Sid picks him up and kisses him on the forehead.)

Above all, Doris longs for a touch of the romance missing from her life, some sense that there is more to her marriage than the dull day-to-day routine. In one sketch, urged on by a friend who insists that she must keep her husband "intoxicated with romance," must keep changing her personality, Doris strives diligently to create a heady atmosphere of exotic passion. She lights candles and sprays the air with perfume, humming "*l'amour, l'amour, l'amour!*" When Charlie arrives home, his reaction is not exactly what Doris has hoped for:

CAESAR: *I'm in the wrong apartment!* [starts to go, turns back] *No, this is where I live!* [Looks around] *This is where I live?* [Changes his mind] *No!* [Changes again] *But it must be! Sure. I . . . I live here! So why does it look like a Persian slave market? . . .* [He goes to the telephone, dials] *Hello, Pete. Will you call me up? I want to see if I'm home.* [Hangs up, phone rings, he picks it up] *I'm home, all right. Thanks, Pete.*

Doris enters in a satin negligee trimmed with maribou, a diaphanous veil over her face. Clutching a long cigarette holder, she begins her passionate exhortations: "My beloved! Light of my love! Heart of my heart! Man of my golden dreams!" Charlie is surprised but unimpressed ("Come on . . . what's with this getup?"), encouraging Doris to try harder:

COCA: *I am the moon and I'm mysterious. I am the stars and I'm romantic. I am the sky and I'm ethereal.*

CAESAR: *And I'm Charlie Hickenlooper and I'm hungry.*

Clearly, Charlie is not too pleased about coming home to a house that has turned into an Arabian brothel, and a wife dressed like Scheherazade. Spurned and humiliated, Doris changes from sensuous demimondaine to indignant hausfrau:

COCA: *I'm only trying to bring a little romance and adventure into our lives! I'm tired of being taken for granted! What happened to the glamour that used to surround us? Where is the excitement of yesterday? Where did our romance disappear?*

CAESAR: *How do I know where you put things? I can't even find my shirts.*

Time and time again, Doris not only attempts to raise the level of their lifestyle, but to actually change their way of life—to alter their "image." And when she begins the process with her own person, the results are an enraged Charlie, responding with alarm and despairing ferocity to the "new look" in wives. In "The New Hair-Do," his reaction of shock and horror at Doris' extreme new coiffure produces this amazing bit of dialogue:

COCA: *Oh, you're ashamed of me! Go ahead, say it! Say it, if you dare!*

CAESAR: *I'm ashamed of you!*

COCA: *Go ahead! Say you're ashamed!*

CAESAR: *I said it!*

COCA: *Say it as though you mean it!*

CAESAR: [With deep conviction] *I'm ashamed of you!*

COCA: *Do you realize what you said?*

CAESAR: *What?*

COCA: *You said you're ashamed of me!*

CAESAR: *I said that?*

COCA: [Sticking her head in front of him] *Yes, you did!*

CAESAR: *You asked me to say it.*

COCA: *You don't have to do everything you're told to do.*

One of Charlie Hickenlooper's most overwrought reactions occurs when Doris takes it on herself to raise their social status by putting a deposit on a new house. As usual, he tries to cope with the situation by employing a barrage of words as his weapon. And as usual, the barrage is stopped by Doris' own weapon: a single well-aimed sentence, like a poisoned dart that unerringly finds its target:

CAESAR: *You're moving? Good. And I'll come and visit you every Sunday. I like this house! [Rises] I like it. I like everything about it. I like this house. I'm used to it. I like it. You understand? It took me two years to memorize this telephone number and I finally learned it and I like the telephone number. I like it. I'm used to this house. I know which step is missing in the stairway and my leg is healed. I know how to jump over it. I just got used to the rhythm of the dripping faucet. It puts me to sleep and I don't want to get used to a new drip. I'm going to stay here until the paint comes off the ceiling, the walls come tumbling down, and the floor disintegrates underneath us.*

COCA: [A fraction of a pause] All right. I can wait two weeks.

Doris and Charlie's quarrels are frequent and noisy, but they have a quality far different from the blatant shouting matches of other television couples. The quarrels have their roots in reality—a missed appointment, a miscalculated word, an injured party—but the observant wit of the writers and the performing genius of Caesar and Coca take the heated words to a comic level several notches *above* reality.

Caesar, in particular, is given many opportunities to exercise his ability to take an ordinary situation to manic heights. When Coca drives him insane by insisting on changing her clothing repeatedly just before a theater engagement, he explodes with a comic fury that takes a physical turn—he begins tearing off his clothes:

If you can change, I can change! I don't like the handkerchief. It doesn't match my eyes! And the eyes don't match the shoes! And the socks don't go with the jacket! And the jacket don't go with the pants! They're the same! And the shirt doesn't match my hair! [He keeps tearing things off until he's standing in his shorts.]

Another time, Doris and Charlie are preparing a party list, and in discussing the guests they might invite, she accuses him of wanting a Mrs. Hopkins to come so that he can flirt with her. Charlie is aghast at the accusation, but Doris confronts him with a baleful eye (there could be no eye more baleful than Coca's), and he responds with a marvelous bit of embroidery:

COCA: You know what I mean. You helped her on with her coat.

The Hickenloopers.

CAESAR: [Laughing] I helped her on with her coat! You finally caught me! I admit it! I helped a lady on with her coat! I stand before the universe, accused! And I confess . . . I helped a lady on with her coat! Oh, vile deed that I have committed! Woe to me and all those who shall follow after! Let it be known down through eternity that I, Charlie Hickenlooper, helped a lady on with her coat. Send messengers to the far corners of the earth! Tell them to erect their guillotines, to light their witches' fire, for the just punishment of a hideous crime! I helped a lady on with her coat!

COCA: [Forever the last word] You never help me on with my coat.

In "The Poker Game," one of the best of the Hickenlooper sketches, Charlie tries the very same ploy of defusing Doris' anger with mockery. But this time he seems to achieve his goal. Caught by Doris at an all-night poker party after he has forgotten their earlier appointment, he tries to bellow his way out of a bad situation:

CAESAR: [Rising] You win. Behold, the conquering hero. Hail to thee, all powerful! You have vanquished me. I am your captive. You have reached out the iron hand and the velvet glove has smote me in my iniquity! I am shamed into oblivion. You are the ruler. Whatever you say, so shall I do! Mine is not to question why, mine is but to do and drop dead. You are the master. Take me away, O master! Take your slave, and lead him back into the dungeon!

COCA: Oh, no! You're pretty clever, aren't you? Well, I'm not going to have your friends calling me a shrew behind my back. Go ahead, finish the game!

Charlie may win a round or two, but his ravings and rantings at Doris' oppressive attitude toward him are merely a feeble squeak compared to her fury when aroused by Charlie's obtuseness and lapses of judgment. As Doris Hicken-

91

looper in the throes of a giant rage, Imogene Coca is a woman possessed: eyes blazing, active index finger pointing at Charlie's chest like a dagger ready to strike, voice that could be coyly entreating turning suddenly into a hectoring whine. A first-rate example can be found in the same sketch, "The Poker Game," as Doris, having waited for hours in the cold, belabors poor Charlie for his sin:

COCA: *You haven't heard the last of this! You're gonna suffer for this! For every minute I was out in that cold, you're going to have one hour of utter misery! [She backs him up against the wall, her face up against his.] I don't forget these things, you know! I have a very good memory! [He starts to slide down the wall. She follows him.] And it's not as though this is the first time it happened! This happens all the time! But it's not going to happen again! I can tell you that!*

Later in the sketch, when the marathon poker game has started again, Doris expands on her tale of misery and woe:

COCA: *I stood on that cold, windy corner for four hours. People stared at me. Finally, a policeman came over and said: "What are you doing, standing on this corner for four hours? You must be frozen stiff." I couldn't tell him I was waiting for my husband. I was too humiliated. So I told him I had amnesia. He wanted to take me to the police station. I'll never know how I got out of that patrol car. There I stood, on that corner, all dressed up, with a corsage of orchids. People thought I was selling flowers. I made two fifty. Much good it did me. Hungry, cold, deserted by my husband. . . .*

Usually, the Hickenlooper quarrel is a game of parry and thrust, with each trying to find the other's most vulnerable spot. But though each demands an apology from the other, somehow Doris always ends up with the advantage—and the last word. At the height of one fierce battle, Charlie accuses her of stubbornness. They assume a nose-to-nose stance, one which many viewers remember with pleasure:

CAESAR: *You and your stubbornness! Stubborn, stubborn, stubb-or-in! Why don't you apologize? Admit that you're wrong. Apologize!*
COCA: *You apologize!*
CAESAR: *I should apologize? For what? What?*
COCA: *You know.*
CAESAR: *I'll never apologize for that!*

In a restaurant, Doris suspects every man of flirting with her.

The Hickenloopers in a Paris restaurant.

COCA: *I think it's absolutely ridiculous for two grown-up people to act like children. Let's talk it over, discuss the whole thing from your point of view, look at the situation like adult people, and then we'll find out that I've been right all the time!*

One Hickenlooper sketch, "The Birthday Present," involved the couple in a familiar situation: he has forgotten to buy her a birthday gift and she is consumed with rage and bitter disappointment. She becomes even angrier when he hands her a present—and promptly falls asleep. She pushes him awake and continues to harangue him about his indifferent behavior. She finally manages to get a perfunctory rendition of "Happy Birthday" out of him. When she complains, he gives her an emotion-charged rendition of the song to the melody of Handel's "Hallelujah" chorus. A typical exchange follows:

COCA: *You never treated me like this before we were married.*

CAESAR: *That's the biggest lie of all!*

93

What a lie! I always treated you rotten—that's the one thing about our marriage. It's honest and aboveboard. You knew what you were getting into. I'm a rat.

Still upset, Doris asks him for his definition of marriage.

CAESAR: Okay, I'll tell you. Marriage is—[He twitches and shudders, groans piteously, and then makes a terrible face]—Oooh, that's what marriage is.

COCA: To you marriage is like a hotel. Eat and sleep. [She pulls out her handkerchief and bursts into tears.] I don't ask much—a little romance—a little attention—some affection now and then.

CAESAR: Please, Doris, don't cry. I understand you. You got troubles. [She cries louder.] You have a problem. Please don't cry. Don't cry. I know it's not easy for you. I know your problem—you're a crazy nut! You cry about anything.

In another sketch, "The Scented Letter," Doris discovers a perfumed letter for Charlie and naturally suspects the worst. Charlie tries to take the advantage by a show of outraged innocence—and this time it *almost* works:

CAESAR: I know what you're thinking. Well, it's not what you think! We're married ten years and you're still thinking! Well, stop thinking! You ought to be ashamed of what you're thinking! If I thought you were thinking what I think you're thinking, you ought to apologize! Say you're sorry! Go on! Apologize! Apologize!

COCA: [Crushed] I apologize! [Suddenly] What am I apologizing for? You get a letter scented with magnolias from a tall, blue-eyed blonde that you met in some bar while you were having a drink, and I apologize!

When the Hickenloopers aren't quarreling over their own differences of opinion, they are often involved in contretemps with their friends and neighbors. In "A Very Important Matter," Doris gets furious with a neighbor who insists on leaving her garbage outside the incinerator. She loses her temper with the neighbor ("Keep your greasy chicken bones out of my hallway!") and tries to get Charlie on her side in the fight. Soon the neighbor's husband (Carl Reiner) is embroiled in the matter—and a full-scale war erupts, with pails of garbage as weapons. Beginning as a timid soul, Charlie becomes an embattled war leader, making brave speeches to his army of one. As Doris prepares to toss everything they own into the fray, Charlie stops her:

CAESAR: Wait a minute. Not so fast. You don't just go and throw garbage. You've got to know why. We can't afford to lose this fight. This isn't just for us. It's for everyone in the building! Everyone in the city! Everyone in this country! It's a fight of the decent people of the world against the slobs who throw garbage in the halls! I tell you we've got to win! When I tell you, open the door! Onward to victory! [Coca opens the door and a pile of garbage hits them.]

On another occasion, the Hickenloopers are entertaining guests, with Charlie playing the perfect host. A hitch develops when the evening's honored guest, Charlie's boss, fails to appear. But he telephones Charlie, giving Sid Caesar the opportunity for a monologue that cheerfully parodies every attempt to provide complicated directions for a lost visitor:

CAESAR: Where are you now? You took Market . . . that's right. Then you turned into . . . that's right . . . that's right . . . that's right . . . that's right . . . that's where you made your mistake. It's a natural mistake. I'll tell you what to do. Get back on the ferry. When you get across, follow the car tracks until you hit the

The Hickenloopers in "The Birthday Present."

94

The Hickenloopers in "A Very Important Matter."

fourth traffic light. Then you come to the bridge. Follow that till you get to a big tunnel. Don't take it. Go up to the ramp until you hit the boulevard. Then head for Mopack... You know where Mopack is? Well, you better stick to the highway....

Later, when his desperate boss calls again, Charlie says: "Where are you now? ... Well, you're an American citizen ... they've got to let you back in the country!"

Several of the Hickenlooper sketches over the run of "Your Show of Shows" professed to show how the Hickenloopers met. According to the sketch "Memories," Doris was Doris even then. Discussing persistent beau Charlie with her friend Beatrice, Doris is indisputably blunt:

COCA: *I don't like him. I don't want to talk about him. I don't want to look at him. I don't want to put up with him. I can go out with other people. I went out* before. *I'll go out again. He's not the only man in the world. And I wouldn't go out with him even if he were.*

BEATRICE: *But Doris, why? What happened? What did he do?*

COCA: *I don't need him. I can't stand him. I don't want him. You can have him. He's too dumb for me.*

Yet despite this, they somehow make it to the justice of the peace where, before the ceremony begins, Charlie tries to tell Doris all his many faults. He expounds on them at length—his snoring, his temper, his forgetfulness, his cheapness—and they form a rather repellent portrait.

COCA: [*All-forgiving*] *Well, that's not so bad. We're only human. I have my faults, too. I can't cook—*

CAESAR: [*Throws up his hands*] *That's all! I don't have to hear any more! The* marriage is off! I'm sorry! That I don't have to put up with! That's another fault I have . . . I like to eat! I like a good meal, boy! That's very important! I gotta eat! [*Doris bursts into tears.*]

We'll leave Doris and Charlie Hickenlooper in a situation dear to the hearts of purveyors of situation comedy on television. It appears that there's a burglar in the house, and where formula comedy would dictate that the terrified couple shriek and stumble over the furniture, the "Show of Shows" writers approach the dilemma differently. As Doris shrilly demands that he catch the burglar, Charlie tries to treat the disturbance like a broken faucet:

CAESAR: *I had a very hard time at the office with all the aggravation. I had to go over the books . . . we took inventory. Why do I have to come home and do all those little jobs around the house? [There*

Caesar and Coca as Samson and Delilah.

is a crash in the kitchen and Coca screams.] Okay, I'll get him. Gimme the gun.

COCA: We haven't got a gun.

CAESAR: You never have anything in the house I want. Fruit ... toothpaste ... a gun. You never have them when I need them.

While the burglar ransacks the kitchen, Charlie calls the police:

CAESAR: [Yells to kitchen] Did you hear that in the kitchen there, Mr. Burglar? I called the police! You're in trouble now. The police are coming! They'll catch you! Then they'll take your fingerprints, and they'll put a number on you and take a picture. One like this [posing] and one like this [posing again], and the judge will be very mad at you.

The Hickenloopers end up piling furniture against the door, and seizing any weapons they can find to subdue the burglar, who never materializes.

Occasionally, the Caesar-Coca combination veered from one of the weekly formulas. On the very first program, Caesar played a hairy Samson to Coca's scheming, grimly determined Delilah. ("Excuse me, there's a crazy woman after me with a pair of scissors.") There was also the delightful "Tramp Ballet," which had the two as gaily scampering hoboes; their winning English music hall rendition of "Lily of Laguna"; their frisky cavorting as circus clowns; and on one occasion, a highly risible sketch with Caesar as a put-upon prizefighter and Coca as his relentlessly nagging wife. As Caesar begs her to let him get ready for his big bout ("You know how it is"), Coca begins a litany of lifelong grievances:

COCA: I know how it is, all right. I know how it's been from the day I married you. You're gone all day while I wash the dishes, scrub the floors, and polish the furniture, and then when you finally do come home from work, you're always tired! [Mocking] "I got a headache! I got a toothache! I got a concussion!"

And on she goes, her voice virtually riveting him to the table:

COCA: Look at you. You promised to call me and you didn't call me. I wouldn't care if you didn't call me if you didn't promise to call me. [Long pause] Why didn't you call me? Next time don't promise if you're not going to keep your promise. That's all I ask, don't promise. [Another pause, and she is off again] Why did you promise?

In anguish, Caesar hopes his opponent will hit him "right in the ears—one shot in the ear and I won't hear that voice." Even when he explodes in a rage, she persists with demonic intensity:

COCA: This place is a mess. How can you be such a slob? [Picks up towel] Always picking up after him. . . . He can live in filth, this man. . . .

Finally, Caesar is taken away by his trainer and manager, boxing his shadow like a mechanical doll, rendered useless by his gorgon of a wife. Of course she has the last word: "Don't forget to come home right after work and bring home a loaf of white bread. . . . Ah, he'll forget . . . he never remembers anything."

One of the most artful of their non-formula duologues was their depiction of two lions in a zoo. We come upon them roaring, primping, scratching their ears, and crossing their "paws" with pantomimic skill. Soon they are exchanging compliments:

CAESAR: You have beautiful fangs. And for a girl, you have a beautiful moustache. [He fluffs his mane.]

COCA: Your mane is gorgeous.

CAESAR: It's my crowning glory.

A moment later, they are complaining about the food:

Caesar and Coca as a boxer and his wife.

COCA: *Did you eat that meal they gave us last night?*

CAESAR: *Don't remind me. Where did they get the idea lions only liked to eat raw meat? I'm dying for a green salad or some creamed cauliflower.*

COCA: *Sounds good. And a nice caramel custard.*

After casting a few aspersions on other residents of the zoo (including the "dirty white coat" of the polar bears), they comment on the keepers:

COCA: *Who's your favorite keeper? Do you like the young keeper or the old keeper?*

CAESAR: *I like the fat keeper. He has such nice blue eyes. A delicious-looking man.*

COCA: *Looks like quite a dish.*

Together, especially in the Hickenlooper sketches, Caesar and Coca complemented each other in dozens of subtle and skillful ways. The contrast in their sizes was used to comical effect: Caesar the ungainly oaf towering above the petite Coca. But whereas many comedy teams would settle on this Mutt and Jeff effect for most of their laughs, Caesar and Coca acknowledged it and built on it. Backed by writers who understood their special qualities, they added irony: the overbearing man bested by the tenacious little woman. They added satire: the culture-crazy, experience-hungry wife dragging her mundane husband along with her on the road to enlightenment. Above all, they added a humanity drawn from their own lives and those of the writers who created the sketches. In the heat of a quarrel, Caesar's voice would begin to thunder, and he would seem to be expressing a truism that sadly applies to many marriages: "You know what, Doris? I'm for you—you're for me, but we're not for each other."

Coca and Caesar as two lions in a zoo.

"When you wrote for Caesar and Coca," says Mel Tolkin, "you used everything you knew: all your life, every movie you ever saw, every book you ever read. You made total use of all your experiences."

After "Your Show of Shows," the situations of the Hickenlooper sketches became staple ingredients for many of the cookie-cutter situation comedies. But the Hickenloopers remained true to themselves. Charlie Hickenlooper's suffering and indignation; Doris Hickenlooper's striving, her fussing and fuming—these were identifiable human attitudes, tilted just enough to induce hearty laughter in the audience. And we laughed. Oh, how we laughed.

7

The Golden Silence

As THE BATTLING Hickenloopers or the platitudinous couple of the cliché sketches, Caesar and Coca confronted the stumbling blocks and booby traps (often self-imposed) along life's highway and managed to survive the trip reasonably intact. In these sketches, they were armed with words, torrents of words they could unleash at the world or at each other. Caesar would expose his pain and vulnerability with bursts of ferocity, and Coca could retaliate with tirades in which the words were like poison-tipped arrows.

Shorn of words, they proved equally adept in the series of pantomimes they performed on "Your Show of Shows." Masters of the pantomimic art, they were able to take fundamental situations and, with facial expressions and bodily movements, make them entirely clear to the audience. Without taking their pantomimes to the symbolic level of Marcel Marceau, they nevertheless portrayed two readily identifiable people, married or strangers, who encounter various dilemmas, problems, and challenges every day.*

A pantomime might involve the simplest of situations. On one occasion, as strangers confronting each other in the subway, Caesar and Coca wage a ferocious battle for a seat, with Coca using all the tricks at her command. In the station, they vibrate in unison as the train pulls up to the platform. Grappling together at the open door, they plunge into the train, only to find all seats taken. (As expected, Caesar bears the brunt of the violence, getting hit by the closing door and crashing against a hapless passenger as he fights for a seat). When a seat becomes vacant, the Caesar-Coca imbroglio gets under way. They push against each other, with neither giving an inch, until Caesar succeeds in crashing through the barrier to the seat. In a series of maneuvers to get the seat, Coca acts coyly seductive, appeals to Caesar's sense of pity by feigning a terrible backache and aching feet, and finally resorts to making a dramatic appeal to the other passengers. When Sid gets up to make a rebuttal speech, a third party takes the seat. Stepping on passengers' toes as a kind of revenge, Caesar and Coca leave the train.

On another occasion, Caesar and Coca attend a concert at Carnegie Hall. Strangers with nothing in common but a love of music, they take adjacent seats, straining to give themselves over to the music. As the music begins, Caesar is immediately transported, getting so deep into the music that he starts to clutch Coca's hand. When he realizes what he is doing, he reacts with dismay, tossing her hand away like a lighted grenade.

* One of the program's writers, Tony Webster, has remarked: "When Sid picks up anything in pantomime, you can take a ruler and measure it. He had a perfect sense of pantomime. You could put the real object into the imaginary place and it would fit."

But in a moment, the music has him back in a rhapsodic trance. This time he begins to rub Coca's shoulder, and the oblivious Coca reciprocates. The music builds in intensity, and in an excess of emotion, Coca begins to beat her legs, and an overcome Caesar takes her hands and beats his own chest with them.

Now the music turns romantic, and they fall into a sentimental haze. But the music quickly becomes furious again, and Caesar begins to behave like the Frankenstein monster on a rampage, gnashing his teeth and distorting his face. Coca responds in kind, and they begin struggling ferociously. (Coca even manages to throw Caesar onto his chair on an exact musical cue!) The love theme returns, and they are ardent again.

Once more, the music turns violent, a cacophony of clashing cymbals and blaring brass. Violence erupts, hilariously. Caesar takes Coca's hat and tears it to pieces. Coca rips his suit, tears his shirt to shreds, and flings the remnants on the floor. At the end of the music, both applaud, nonchalantly pick up the remains of their wardrobe, and walk away from each other, having enjoyed a rare musical experience.

One of their best-remembered pantomimes also involved music. In "Music Recital," he is the violinist, she the pianist in a marvelously timed display of comical mishaps. They enter in traditional fashion, bowing to the audience and to each other, and proceed to the recital. Only there are a few setbacks before they play. In succession: (1) Coca tries to adjust the piano stool, and the top flies off; (2) inadvertently, she manages to drop the open piano top on Caesar's hand—not once but twice—permitting him to register pain eloquently; (3) Caesar somehow steps on his violin, and when he gets a replace-

ment from the wings, the second violin collapses in his hand. As another tactic designed to exasperate Caesar, Coca insists on slowly removing all her jewelry—rings, necklace, tiara, etc.—before playing.

Even when they finally begin, poor Caesar is still disaster-prone. He not only breaks a string in his violin but stabs himself with his bow, forcing Coca to perform quick surgery on the spot. He is also hit in the eye with something thrown from the audience. Three times, they attempt to tune up, making an unruly audience even unrulier. Caesar starts to play "Humoresque," but a swift, dirty look from Coca gets him back on the opening of "Czardas."

When Caesar plays a few excruciatingly wrong notes, people in the audience begin throwing things at them. Obviously no stranger to this scene, Caesar manages to avoid the objects with some dexterous ducking, but Coca is hit. They continue playing, warding off flying objects and ending with a rousing chorus of "Czardas." They bow with dignity, only to get hit in the face in a very undignified fashion. They exit, dodging debris all the way.

Many of the pantomimes involved Caesar and Coca as a married couple in pursuit of simple pleasures—and finding nothing quite as simple as they had expected. In "Coney Island," they seek a day of fun at the amusement park, with mixed results. It begins with a test of strength for Caesar: he must swing a heavy mallet, causing a rising disc to strike the bell at the top of a high column. Predictably, he misses, but not so predictably, Coca *also* misses when she tries to do the same. In the Hall of Mirrors, they react to appearing alternately fat and skinny, and Coca has her skirt blown by a wind machine in the Fun House. Caesar buys tickets for the shooting gallery but misses the target every time. Coca, a bit confused, points her rifle at him and they make a hasty retreat.

An encounter in a subway.

In the best segment of the sketch, Sid and Imogene take a nerve-jangling ride on a roller coaster. Using their pantomimic skills to the fullest, they express the giddiness, fear, and exhilaration of the ride. They convey expertly the sense of being tossed about in a roller-coaster car as it lurches over one steep hill after another. Caesar has enjoyed himself, but a badly shaken Coca refuses to take a second ride. They proceed to an orgy of eating, downing hot dogs, popcorn, ice cream cones, sodas, and corn in rapid succession. Coca becomes progressively sicker, but Sid happily munches his way from course to course. Only at the end, when he looks at Coca, then looks at his stomach, does he, too, become ill. Sick, sated, and possibly happy, the two stagger offstage.

In another sketch, with perhaps not so strenuous a good time in mind, Caesar and Coca go out for a pleasant day in the park. Entering the park, they spot some pigeons and decide to feed them. Sid takes a huge bag of feed down from his shoulder, and they proceed to sprinkle some for the birds. Amused, he makes one pigeon come up to his hand for the feed, and insists that Imogene do the same. He puts some feed on her hand but a perverse pigeon alights on his head instead.

Off they go to the zoo, where they gaze with pleasure at the lions, elephants, hippos, and monkeys. Coca imitates the monkey, and Caesar takes a picture of her. After he takes a picture of the monkey, he and Coca pose proudly, and the monkey apparently takes a picture of *them!*

Next stop: the carousel. They ride around twice, but the second time Caesar's horse, obviously with a mind of its own, begins to buck and rides off with him. Shaken by the double ride, they leave the carousel a little the worse for wear.

Finally, they take a boat out on the lake. In a series of precisely timed moves, they try to arrange themselves and their oars so that they will be rowing together, rather than in opposite directions. No luck. Every time they turn, they find themselves back to back! Attempting to leave the boat, the two end up in the lake instead. Wet and chagrined, they climb up on the dock, certain to remember their day in the park.

On dry land, our pantomimic couple continue their pursuit of Simple Fun. On their way to a cocktail party after the theater, they set themselves an awesome task: finding a taxi. Chattering about the show they've just seen, they notice that it's raining and decide to hail a cab. One goes by without stopping. Another goes by—and splashes them. A third cab goes by and sideswipes Caesar.

Annoyed, Caesar steps into the street, and puts his hand up to stop an approaching cab. The cab runs into him, apparently only breaking his pocket watch. A little *more* annoyed, Caesar lies down in the street while Coca tries to hail a cab. Once again, the cab runs over him. He gets up, feels himself all over, and looks at his watch, which is now running! "Thank you," he shouts after the departing cabbie.

Still no cab. Now Coca decides to use her own tactics. She gets a cab to stop by flirting with the driver, but when she starts getting too involved in her performance, Caesar intervenes and gets punched for his pains. Suddenly Coca remembers that she has an umbrella. She takes it out of her purse, and in three swift gestures, unzips it, untelescopes it, and raises it against the rain. She and Caesar get under the umbrella, but it isn't large enough for the two of them. They exit together.

Slightly damp, Caesar and Coca arrive at the "Cocktail Party." He is evidently reluctant to attend, since Coca forces him to raise his arm to knock at the door. They are greeted effusively by their hostess and urged to mingle. And mingle they do, especially Caesar, who immedi-

Caesar and Coca emerging from the carousel at Coney Island Amusement Park.

ately latches onto an attractive guest. As he chats with her amiably, his face wreathed in a fatuous smile, Coca saunters over and listens. She gets in front of Caesar and clearly mouths the words, *"He's my husband!"*

Coca manages to lead Caesar away and introduces him to a scholarly-looking gentleman. Uninterested, he spills a cocktail on himself and wends his way back to the attractive lady. Again, Coca joins them, and again she brings Caesar back to the cocktail table. Glumly, he eats a canape and shakes hands with the scholarly gentleman. Spotting the lady again, he uses a new ploy: he introduces Coca to Handsome Harry, and once she begins an animated conversation, he saunters off to the lady. This time, however, he becomes concerned about how well Coca and Handsome Harry are hitting it off. When Coca begins to dance with Harry,

*At a cocktail party, wife Coca
clearly disapproves of husband
Caesar's excess of party spirits.*

Caesar also moves onto the floor, holding an imaginary woman in his arms. Skillfully, he manages to get next to Coca and dance off with her into the night. She leaves with him—but under protest.

Another time, Sid and Imogene decide to have their very own get-together. "Let's Have a Party" begins with a splendid piece of pantomimic buffoonery as Caesar mixes a punch. He puts in several ingredients, tastes it, and finds it too strong. He adds a few more ingredients, tastes it again—and finds that his tongue has gotten caught between his teeth! He recovers and adds still more ingredients: several eggs, a sliced banana—and onions. The onions make him cry.

Coca enters to remind him that their guests will be arriving soon. She asks him to help her with her dress, and he proceeds to go through elaborate maneuvers. He hooks up the side, buttons up the back all the way over her head, takes

a screw driver and screws down a couple of loose ends, and applies a few nails with a cobbler's hammer.

The guests begin to arrive, and Caesar and Coca greet them at the door. Sid collects the coats and places them on Imogene's arm. Bending low under the load, she takes them across the room and places them on the couch. Sid offers a drink to a man, who gulps it down and topples over abruptly. Sid picks him up and puts him on the pile of coats. The guests are obviously famished, since plates of canapes disappear as quickly as they are prepared. Sid fixes them at a furious pace, slapping them together with abandon. For a moment, he is the Master of Canapes.

The pace accelerates. A guest guzzles his drink, and everyone watches as he flies around the room—he finally falls and they toss him on the couch. The doorbell rings, and a stranger enters. They give him a drink; he wobbles back and forth and finally falls. He is tossed out of the door unceremoniously. Finally, exhausted and surrounded by debris, Caesar and Coca hint at the lateness of the hour— and push everyone out. Alone at last, they begin to make drinks for themselves —and face the aftermath of a really rousing party.

Skillfully performed by Caesar and Coca, these pantomimes became a popular regular feature of "Your Show of Shows." The range of situations was familiar to everyone: attending a singles dance; coping with dire complications at a picnic; watching a parade; bringing a new baby home from the hospital; trying out a new camera; teaching a wife to drive, and many others. Like the best pantomimes, they distilled life's experiences, before they could be shaped, distorted, or colored by words.

As expert as the Caesar-Coca pantomimes were, the company's pantomimic gifts reached their zenith in the series of take-offs of silent movies. Without burlesquing or demeaning the achievements of the silent screen, "Your Show of Shows" happily re-created the extravagant attitudes and gestures—and even more extravagant emotions—of the movies in their early years. Wisely, the program chose not to mimic the classic comedy styles of Charlie Chaplin or Buster Keaton, confining itself to the basic dramatic situations involving unbridled passion, base treachery, naked deceit, and—for a change of pace—familial devotion. With Sid Caesar, Imogene Coca, Carl Reiner, and Howie Morris at their peak, the silent movie pantomimes presented—with just the right note of comic exaggeration—a parade of self-sacrificing or wicked wives, noble or straying husbands, leering vamps, abandoned children, ardent lovers, and an assortment of doom-predicting, head-shaking, or sympathetic parents, friends, and confidants.

Many of the silent movies of the twenties had reflected the double standard of the time: on one side was the hell-bent hedonism of the Jazz Age, replete with madly dancing flappers, gin flasks, and a general air of live-for-today; on the other side were the cautionary warnings of zealous moralists who insisted that the obsession with sex, wealth, and having a good time would end in degradation and disaster. The movies of the day championed both sides: inevitably, scenes of rampant dissipation would be followed by scenes of despair and bitter regret. As Cecil B. DeMille discovered, mixing sin and morality in the same movie gave the producer a heady brew for the box office.

"Your Show of Shows" often mixed the same brew in its very own silent movies. That born victim played so assiduously by Sid Caesar frequently found himself in deep trouble, capsized by a lust for gold, ravaged by an insatiable thirst

During a driving lesson, teacher Caesar registers horror while student Coca registers euphoria.

for hard liquor, or totally destroyed by his burning desire for some tawdry wench. His ruin was usually as complete as his remorse.

The steamy melodrama "A Fool's Fate" is a case in point. We come upon a gala party scene at which Sid and Virginia Curtis are in the midst of celebrating their anniversary. Enter Imogene Coca on the arm of Jack Russell, dressed to the nines (or maybe tens and elevens) of twenties fashion. Caesar spots her and falls into a violent reaction signifying Instant Lust. His arms shake, his head twitches—he seems to have fallen into a giant Mixmaster. Coca is not disinterested: "Who is that man?" she mouths to Russell, her face expressing a frank Coca-style admiration for Caesar. In a moment, she is dancing a quick-step with Caesar, who has already forgotten his marriage vows and is panting after this devastating creature. Despite a warning from friend Carl Reiner, Caesar is

hooked, and when Coca gives him her address, he falls into another paroxysm of desire and delight. (No subdued emotions here.)

Three months later, Caesar is dissipating with Coca. As Caesar sprawls across a chaise longue, Coca, in the silent-film tradition of expressing shameless passion, feeds him grapes, one by one. He plies her with jewels and ardent embraces. In come wife Virginia and their baby with spoilsport Reiner, a surefire double device for bringing the straying Sid back to his home and hearth. Audaciously, Coca vamps Caesar in front of his wife and child, but when she hears that Caesar is broke, she turns him out of her boudoir —ostensibly for good.

A title card reads "Homeless and Hungry" and we see poor Caesar as a park derelict, scrounging for pennies and hungrily eyeing Howie Morris' enormous sandwich. Coca, more overdressed than ever, enters on the arm of an admirer. In

A FOOL'S FATE begins with Sid Caesar and Virginia Curtis celebrating their wedding anniversary.

Enter vamp Imogene Coca on the arm of Jack Russell. Caesar reacts to the dazzling sight of Coca.

He falls into a paroxysm of desire. A quick dance with Coca—and all is lost.

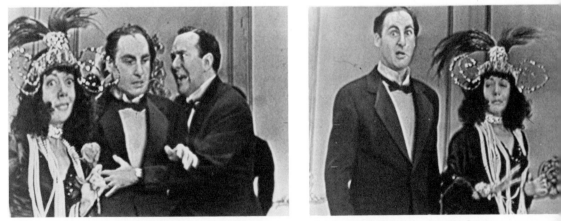

Friend Carl Reiner issues a warning . . . but Caesar is completely hooked. Three months later, Caesar plies Coca with jewels. Reiner pleads with Caesar to return to his wife and baby . . .

... but Coca vamps Caesar shamelessly before his family. Coca learns that Caesar is broke ...

... and doesn't like the idea. "Out you go!" she tells him.

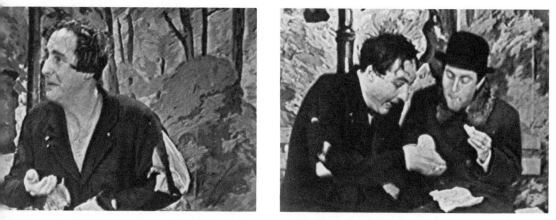

"Homeless and Hungry" Caesar tries to borrow some of Howie Morris' sandwich.
Confronting Coca in the park, he tries to strangle her. Reiner urges Caesar to come home.

But what man could resist a woman like this? Not Caesar, and again he offers her jewels.

Coca, looking decadent. She bites the jewels and finds them wanting.

Home again—but too late. A drunken Caesar pours liquor in his ear. A total wreck, he staggers down the stairs—and falls. Caesar suffers a fatal heart attack. The message is clear.

a rage, Caesar accuses her of ruining his life and tries to strangle her. He is stopped by Reiner, who just happens to be passing by, and who reminds him of his wife and baby waiting at home.

Alas, the next title card reads "Under the Spell," and indeed, the luckless Caesar is back with Coca. At her most vampish, she is stretched out on her chaise longue, the very picture of decadence. (Has any comic actress ever looked more hilariously decadent?) This time, however, she is not very keen on his attention. Nastily, she rejects his offer of jewels (grapes are out of season), and throws him out.

"Home Again," the title reads, and as Virginia and Carl watch in horror, an anguished Caesar enters the scene and staggers down the stairs. To avoid recriminations (and to keep the "movie" to a reasonable length), Caesar conveniently suffers a heart attack and expires. To a shattered Virginia, Carl mouths the words, "A Fool's Fate."

Money, not a woman, is the Root of All Evil in the movie "Ticker Mad." Here Caesar is a wealthy man who is all business, no heart. Coming home from the office, he heads directly for his beloved ticker-tape machine, ignoring wife Virginia Curtis, who tries to tell him about daughter Imogene Coca's birthday. After his exasperated wife leaves, a wild-eyed Howie Morris crashes into the room, pushing away the butler who is struggling with him. "You've ruined me!" he cries, sinking to his knees at Caesar's well-shod feet. Cold and unaffected, Caesar orders him out.

Now Virginia returns with little Imogene, who wants to play with Daddy. When he ignores her, she playfully dumps a basket of ticker tape on his head. (Coca adds a hint of malice to the mischief, which makes the moment doubly funny.) Caesar is angry, until he becomes aware (finally) that it is his daughter's birthday. Friend-of-the-family

Carl Reiner gives Imogene a doll, and Virginia gives her a locket. When a birthday cake is wheeled in, the negligent Sid tries to compensate by giving Imogene a tidy bundle of money. Unhappy at his indifference, she throws the money away, making a gesture of disdain that again suggests an adult mind hiding surreptitiously behind all the girlish curls. When everyone leaves, Sid returns to his ticker tape, only to learn to his horror that the stock market has crashed. He is a ruined, broken man! (The silent movie titles were not noted for subtlety. A card reads: "The Hand of Fate.")

Years later, in a soup kitchen, Coca enters as a grown-up young lady. Anxious to do her bit for unfortunates, in her own way, she is followed by a chauffeur carrying a soup tureen. Her job: to ladle out the soup for the derelicts who come to the kitchen. Three men get their soup, then Caesar comes in, a bum in tattered clothing. As he holds up his bowl, Coca looks at him and imagines for a moment she recognizes him. She decides no, it can't be, and ladles out more soup. They continue staring at each other, until Caesar sees the locket and asks her where she got it. "My mother gave it to me," she tells him. Overjoyed, he exclaims: "Look into the locket and you will see my picture. You are my child!" Coca looks in the locket, and she and Caesar have a hysterical reunion, with much kissing and embracing. She plans to take him home with her, when he suddenly suffers a heart attack (heart trouble is apparently an occupational disease of misguided husbands and fathers) and falls to the floor. Coca has one long moment of hand-wringing anguish.

Back in the living room, Caesar wakes up with great difficulty, then realizes that he's been dreaming. (Cut to subtle card: "It was only a dream.") His lesson learned, he is delighted to be back home and to join in celebrating little Imogene's birthday.

But the misery hasn't ended, not in a

movie like "Ticker Mad." Sid spots the ticker-tape machine, and in a flash, he is back, avidly reading the results. It seems that the market has staged a comeback. Returning to his old gruff, self-centered, money-is-king character, he pushes Coca away, the better to concentrate on his investments. His feverish money madness is in full force again. The ticker tape has won, after all!

In "Siren's Spell," Caesar again finds his nemesis in Woman. A sensible and responsible husband and father, he is irked when young son Carl Reiner returns home late one evening and tries to sneak past his parents, carrying his shoes. This is clearly a situation to be handled by Dad. Sending Mother from the room, he proceeds to lecture Carl, only to reel back in a stupor when Carl's breath hits him full force. "You have been drinking!" he accuses Carl, who makes a great show of denying it. (He pantomimes that he was bowling.) But a worse evil than liquor looms when Carl takes out his handkerchief and a garter falls from his pocket. Both Sid and Carl grab at the garter, stretching it in a tug-of-war that ends with it painfully snapping at Sid's hand. "Whose garter is this?" he demands to know. Carl tells him reluctantly, and Sid writes the name in his little book. He is off to visit the wicked lady, evidently unaware of the title card that follows: "The Siren's Web."

In her well-appointed web, Imogene Coca, seductive as ever, a jeweled cigarette holder dangling from her scarlet lips, is clearly enjoying her ill-gotten gains. Languishing on her divan, she sprinkles jewels and money over her body in a marvelous gesture of self-worship. Sid is announced, and Imogene goes off to dress for the occasion. A nervous Sid enters the room, carefully checks his watch against the clock on the table—and waits.

When Imogene returns, posed in the doorway, Sid reacts to her dazzling beauty, her seductive, flirtatious ways.

Giving him her best "come hither" look, she drops a rose in front of him. He picks it up, only to get a thorn in his hand. Getting down to business, he remonstrates about his son, showing her the garter and offering to pay her money to leave his son. He writes out a check and gives it to her, and she puts it in her bosom. He starts to leave, and with the practiced gestures of a master hypnotist, she draws him back to her, step by inexorable step. As they embrace, shocked son Carl enters and tries to tell his father that he has fallen into a trap. Desperately, Carl attempts to lead his father away from Imogene, but her gesture draws *both* men to her side.

This vamp is irresistible. Not only has she lured father and son into her web, but four other men follow them on stage! On this note of high-frequency vamping, the movie ends with the title "Beware the siren's spell. It leads to doom."

In these silent movies, it was not always Sid Caesar who played the fallen angel. Imogene Coca took her turn several times at being the well-meaning but weak victim of the decade's hedonism. In "Dancing Mothers," she plays a married flapper who has to learn the error of her wicked ways.

We meet her as she dances gaily about the room in preparation for her big society wingding. A maid helps her on with her dress as she lights one cigarette after another (a sure sign of decadence). Husband Sid enters with their child, bouncing along in the antic manner that invariably signified happiness in silent films. The child is seeking Mother's attention, but Mother has other things on her mind, mostly her jewelry. Obviously, this kid is neglected—and knows it. Only Sid is willing to play with her—they engage in a dance and a strenuous round of patty-cake. When the child plays with Imogene's pearls, she gets angry and has her taken away by the maid. The child expresses her hurt mutely.

Now Coca and Caesar engage in a

In "The Enchanted Ballerina," a pantomime of a silent movie, impresario Caesar is determined to transform charwoman Coca into a great dancer.

quarrel, which is interrupted by the arrival of the first guests. Sid goes off to tuck in the child and tell her a bedtime story, but Coca is off to her party—and one hell of a good time. At the high point of the festivities, she is dancing atop a table as couples cavort shamelessly. Caesar watches in disgust from a distance, but Coca lures him into doing a Charleston with her. As a man cuts in to dance wildly with Coca, the maid enters with a grim announcement: the baby is sick. They call the doctor.

Too dizzy and wound-up to know what's happening, Coca wants her guests to stay, but Caesar finally gets her to understand that their child is seriously ill. In a split second, beautifully man-

aged, Coca veers from indecent laughter to grief-stricken remorse. The parents kneel at the crib of the stricken child as Dr. Carl Reiner enters hurriedly.

It's now time for Coca's big repentance scene. Abjectly, she promises not to be a dancing mother anymore, though Caesar is loath to forgive her. Dr. Reiner enters to tell them that the child is critically ill and he must send for other equipment. Desperately, Imogene pleads with Sid to forgive her, but he pushes her to the floor. Enter baby, suddenly recovered. In a moment of juvenile wisdom, seeing that they've been quarreling (Mother's being on the floor is a dead giveaway), she goes to Sid and Imogene and joins their hands together. Dr. Reiner returns and sees the child restored to health and now restoring harmony to the household. "It's a miracle!" he cries, as Sid and Imogene kneel at their child's side. The End (one certainly hopes).

Occasionally, one of the silent movies gave Imogene Coca the opportunity to use her skill as a dancer. In "Enchanted Ballerina," she is a blowsy charwoman who is transformed by impresario Sid Caesar into a premier ballerina. Caesar comes to a ballet school run by Howie Morris to find a dancer he can train. Rejecting several applicants, he comes upon Coca, scrub pail and all, and decides that she is the one he's been looking for. Her dance steps are awkward and comical until Caesar reveals his insidious plan: he hypnotizes Coca by dangling a pendant before her eyes. Under his spell, she is a veritable Pavlova who can execute even the most complicated steps.

Coca, transformed from char to star, becomes a desirable woman whom impresario Caesar finds irresistible. He uses his hypnotic pendant to get her to kiss him, but she's really not interested. Much more attractive to her is new dance partner Carl Reiner, who meets Coca and a decidedly cool Caesar at the rehearsal. (Carl Reiner's version of a self-confident ballet dancer is splendid. Few comedians are as expert at conveying the smug egocentricity of an "artiste.")

When Coca and Reiner dance, there is an immediate rapport that promises to extend beyond the dance floor. Caesar is definitely irked, and he uses his pendant to hypnotize Coca back into his power. In a hilarious moment, he overextends himself. He flings the pendant, baseball-style, at Coca, but it strikes Carl instead. Carl rushes to Sid and tries to kiss him but Sid beats him off. When Carl falls to the floor, Imogene rushes to his side. In comes a wizard (guest star Jack Palance) who has his *own* pendant and proceeds to destroy the wicked Caesar with it. In a metaphysical touch, Palance turns around to reveal he is wearing

wings. Coca and Reiner embrace as the title card reads "The spell is broken and love triumphs!"

Two of the most popular of the silent movies on "Your Show of Shows" offered contrasting styles in approach and material. "The Love Bandit" was a hard-breathing romantic melodrama in the Rudolph Valentino tradition, while "The Sewing-Machine Girl" was a tear-streaked melodrama of ill-starred love in a slum factory.

In "The Love Bandit," Caesar appears in Valentino garb as a fiery, romantic, devil-may-care gaucho who is being sought by the police. As the pride of the pampas, he enters the cafe where the local citizens have gathered, his wide-brimmed hat tilted rakishly, a cigarette dangling from his lips. (He is practically wreathed in cigarette smoke.) His appearance is startling—he resembles a Valentino drawn in broad strokes by a talented caricaturist. The image is askew just enough to make it extremely funny.

As he enters, Caesar spots his "wanted" poster on the wall and bursts into sardonic laughter. A rude remark from a cafe patron prompts him to take out his whip and knock the cigarette from the offender's lips. In comes Imogene Coca as a fandango dancer, her eyes blazing as she notices Caesar. To show her contempt (really disguised adoration), she proceeds to do one of her dances—on his hat. But no woman dares to defy him, and in a moment he envelops her in a passionate embrace. She tries to fight him off, and we see only her arms as she beats her fists against his back. A second later, she is surrendering with obvious pleasure, her arms dropping blissfully to her sides. Their love-hate battle resumes. She flings water in his face, then joins him in a hilarious tango. (The intensely ardent expression on their faces is an amusing jab at the dead-pan seriousness with which the tango is usually danced.)

Now the police break in to arrest Caesar. Led by sadistic Carl Reiner, they

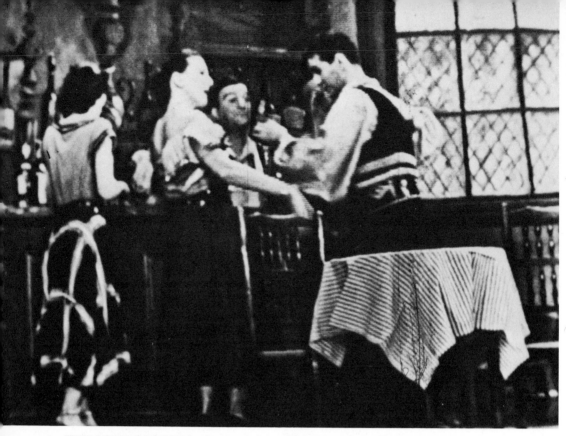

THE LOVE BANDIT *begins as revelers gather at a cafe in Argentina.*

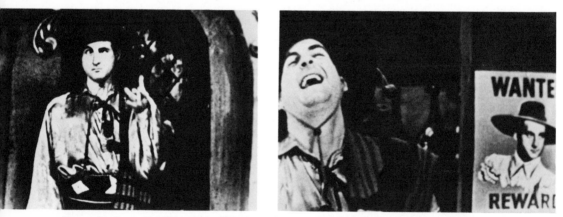

Enter the Love Bandit, wanted by the police . . . and by every woman. The Bandit scoffs at his own "Wanted!" poster, little knowing what lies in store. He reacts (unfavorably) to a remark made by one of the patrons, and being a man of quick action . . . he knocks the cigarette from the patron's mouth with his whip.

Everyone reacts with awe and admiration to the Pride of the Pampas. In comes
La Coca, fiery flamenco dancer, who is always ready to kick up her heels.

The Dancer and the Bandit confront each other defiantly, but with more than a
touch of interest. The Dancer will perform at the drop of a hat (the Bandit's).
She proceeds to stomp on his wide-brim chapeau . . .

. . . and does a good job of it, too. The Bandit is intimidated but also excited
by her beauty. Obviously, there's more than a demolished hat between these two.
The Bandit embraces the reluctant Dancer, as her arms flap in protest . . .
and then drop in total surrender.

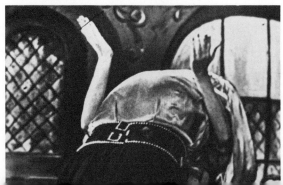

A Tango of Love by the Bandit and the Dancer. Trouble: in come the police, ready to interrogate the Bandit. The Dancer protests.

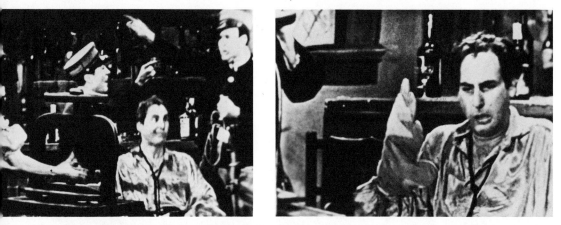

Torture! Sadistic policemen place the Bandit's hand in a vise. The Dancer protests. The Bandit ends up with a hand that changes his glove size.

The dastardly police separate the Bandit and the Dancer. (Hiss!!) A parting for the lovers, two ill-starred people who tangoed their way into each other's hearts.

hold him down as they question him and even torture him for vital information. While Coca looks on in despair, they proceed to place his hand in a vise, crushing his fingers as he refuses to speak.

Caesar emerges with a hand several times its normal size.

Caesar is led away, but not before he and Coca make a frantic and funny attempt to kiss for the last time. Lips

118

straining, they try to reach each other, without success. "The Love Bandit" has been put out of commission, after all.

"The Sewing-Machine Girl," which appeared in the movie Ten From Your Show of Shows, is a sad tale set in the sweatshop where our hapless heroine (Coca) ekes out a small living. In the wretched shop, Coca works with many others, but she has eyes only for Sid Caesar. She and Caesar are in love, and they throw kisses to each other across the sewing machines. When her machine breaks down, he fixes it, then kisses her dainty hand.

Enter the hissable villain, otherwise known as "the boss." A nasty sort, played by Carl Reiner, the boss obviously has his beady eyes set on Coca. He stops at her machine, gets overly familiar, and asks her to go out with him. Sid "accidentally" sticks him with a needle, and the boss leaves. Coca gives an ominous cough, but the work proceeds.

Nothing, of course, stops a dastardly villain, and soon the boss is back, making new advances to Coca. Rebuffed, he angrily orders the workers to "speed up," and soon shirts are flying in every direction. Coca coughs again for good measure.

One very funny piece of business: Lunchtime arrives, and the boss puts up his hand to signify the lunch period. Everyone begins to eat quickly. Caesar tries to get his lunch box open, finally takes out a sandwich—and the boss drops his hand. Lunchtime is over.

Now, as the work speeds up even more, Coca begins to cough loudly and works herself into a state of collapse (a moment handled with wonderful comic dexterity by Coca). Against Sid's protests, the boss carries the collapsed Coca into his office and places her on his sofa. He revives her, and proceeds with an all-out campaign to win her over. He has her try on a fur coat (it's too large); he tries to kiss her (she says never); he shows her jewels (she tries to leave). They struggle, and Imogene screams for help.

Hero Sid rushes in, as a title card reads "I'll fight for your honor." In his eagerness to save Coca, he almost knocks her over. He raises his fists to Carl, but Carl, in a surprise move that triggers laughter, simply hits Sid on the head, and he falls. Imogene rushes to pummel Carl, but Sid is soon back on his feet, ready for round two. Again Carl hits him on the head; again a surprised Sid collapses.

Now tragedy strikes. Coca has a coughing attack that is clearly going to be fatal. Everyone tries to revive her—to no avail. "He killed her!" Sid cries, as all the workers point accusing fingers at the cringing villain. The workers kneel, as poor Imogene is raised to her heavenly reward, a beatific smile on her face. Sid says (and a title card reads): "Farewell, my little sewing-machine girl." Everyone grieves. Cut to card: The End.

Many other silent movies were performed on "Your Show of Shows." They were a popular feature of the program, and rightly so. Ingratiating and funny, never stooping to mock an original art form, they combined the formidable pantomimic skills of the players with a clear affection for the circumscribed world of the silent movie.

As we will see in the next chapter, this same affection extended to the program's full-scale satires of contemporary movies and movie genres. But silent or sound, the result was our grateful laughter.

8

Satire Is What Opens on Saturday Night

It's a FAMILIAR Broadway dictum that satire is what *closes* on Saturday night. The conventional wisdom is that spoofs of current fads, mores, or attitudes turn theatergoers off. Throw poison-dipped darts at sacred cows—personalities, institutions, or ideas—and you may find the darts have boomeranged and are imbedded in your own back.

Well, many a satirical play *has* closed on Saturday night (probably because it was *bad* satire), but others, including some of the better comedies of George S. Kaufman and Moss Hart, have succeeded. And though satire has never been exactly widespread in the American theater, it has not been entirely neglected either.

In the bland, careful world of television, however, satire has always been a rarity. In recent years, such programs as "That Was the Week That Was," "Laugh-In," and "Saturday Night" have offered broad satire, sometimes sharply funny, often heavy-handed, on events of the day. Satirical humor has sprouted occasionally on public television stations, with programs like the sometimes witty "Great American Dream Machine." But with the conspicuous exception of Carol Burnett, who has managed some expert and funny film spoofs, most "satire" on television has taken the form of knockabout slapstick versions of current or classic movies, devoid of wit, point, or subtlety and performed by comedians with little respect or affection for their source material.

Not so "Your Show of Shows." At a time when the mold was being cast for the "I-Love-Lucy-Make-Room-for-Daddy-Father-Knows-Best" situation comedies that inundated television in the fifties, at a time when Milton Berle in drag was the model for television humor, at a time when watching wrestling on television was a popular spectator sport, "Your Show of Shows" took a decisive step in the direction of turning the "boob tube" into a reasonably adult medium. It began to offer weekly satires, not only on the familiar genres of movie history and the most popular contemporary films—but (heaven help the NBC network!) on *foreign* movies as well. For audiences accustomed to televised bowling, Pinky Lee, and Ricky Ricardo, it was a jolt to view takeoffs on *The Blue Angel, Grand Illusion*, and the films of Anna Magnani.

Given the credentials and the inclina-

"From Here to Obscurity": Caesar and Coca doing a takeoff on the famous beach scene in From Here to Eternity.

tions of the people involved in turning out "Your Show of Shows," satire was inevitable. Much of Max Liebman's material for his shows at Tamiment had turned on mocking fads and foibles of the day. The "Show of Shows" writers, several of them Tamiment graduates, were young, bright, and irreverent people who watched classic movies in the Museum of Modern Art auditorium and attended showings of the latest successful films. Certified movie buffs, they recognized the familiar and somewhat shopworn conventions that made movies

eternally popular, and with affection (and perhaps a touch of malice), they began to satirize these conventions on "Your Show of Shows." The spoofs of American and foreign movies became a staple feature of the program.

Since the players on "Your Show of Shows" were musically gifted, it is not surprising that the movie musical became one of the most often repeated targets for satire. The trappings of the movie musical were familiar to every audience: the endearingly foolish plots, the lush orchestra music wafting in from nowhere, the simple failure-to-success formula of the situations. As satirized on "Your Show of Shows," these trappings were duplicated with loving care but with the right amount of comic exaggeration. The result was the most skilled and certainly the funniest satirical material that has ever appeared on television.

One of the best of the group was a spoof of the beloved backstage musical, here called "Broadway Rhapsody." In the hallowed tradition of *42nd Street*, Sid Caesar played Larry Crane, the manic director desperately trying to "put on a show" against insurmountable odds. As he gets his shoes shined, takes a haircut, and even has a tooth pulled, he rants on about the production:

CAESAR: *I got a new idea for a jungle set. Buzzy, get the Hawaiian number ready. I wanna see how it looks. Joe, get me some black coffee. . . .*

Frantic when he's told that his leading lady refuses to show up ("All I wanna do is put a smile on the map of America, but they won't let me!"), he turns, at Howie Morris's suggestion, to a kid in the chorus named Mary Stumbler (Coca). Told that she must learn the leading role in only a few short days, Mary, all wide-eyed innocence, gives way to panic:

COCA: *[Breathless] Oh, Buzzy! I don't think I can do it! I'm scared! I can't sing for Mr. Crane, for the lead in the show! I can't do it it! I'm just a little chorus girl! My voice will crack! I'll forget the lyrics! I can't sing for Mr. Crane! [Suddenly the voice of authority, to the pianist] Key of C, please, and not too fast.*

Director Crane takes the "little chorus girl" in tow and begins to put her through the most grueling paces. Working her and the eternally "klutzy" chorus girls to exhaustion, he bellows at them in the best Warner Baxter manner: "Put a little life into it! A little pep! A little zip!" When Mary's friend Buzzy protests at his rough treatment, Crane considers the matter briefly:

CAESAR: *Yeah, you're right. Okay, kids. Take a rest. [He pauses for a second, then] Okay, rest is over! This time when you jump in the air, stay there a while!*

He finally confronts a prostrate Mary, mincing no words as he exhorts her to get on her feet and give the performance of her life: "You want to be a star, don't you? Well, this is what it means! Hard work! And lots of heartbreak! And lots of sacrifice! And lots of pain and misery!" Mary moans that she cannot go on, but when Crane turns to find a substitute, she is right up there, doing her routine: "Rhythm, rhythm, rhythm!"

A problem: The rich banker has withdrawn his money from the show. The solution: Enter J. Evans Worcestershire (Carl Reiner), the mayonnaise king, who insists he'll back the show only if his dumb girlfriend Jacqueline Moran becomes the star. Does Crane hesitate at the thought of giving Mary's role to a novice? Does he even blink once at his treachery?

MORRIS: *But, Larry, what about Mary? She'll be brokenhearted.*
CAESAR: *There's a broken heart for every light on Broadway.*

Crane breaks the bad news to Mary in his own inimitable way: "A big mayonnaise man came in and offered me a lot of lettuce. Fifty thousand dollars, and that's a lot of cabbage. And he wants his tomato in the show." Mary is bitter— "Your heart is nothing but a big spotlight shining on Larry Crane!"—but Crane is adamant: "Show business is show business."

On opening night, Crane cannot bear the amateurish squeaking of Jacqueline Moran, tosses her out, and asks Mary to return to the cast. Of course he must return the money to Worcestershire, leaving him without a show. True to the grand and glorious tradition, everyone offers to chip in: the old doorman saving his money for an operation ("I don't mind dying if it's for a good cause"), the girls in the chorus. ("All you kids chipping in like this . . . it . . . it's not enough. Nine dollars and thirty-seven cents. That won't pay for the costumes.")

All ends well, however, when it turns out that J. Evans Worcestershire is actually Mary's father! The show goes on, but when Mary has her cue, she panics again and refuses to go onstage. In one swift and inspired move, Crane swings at her and sends her reeling onto the stage. She holds her hand over her mouth, sees the audience, and bursts into song, revealing three blacked-out teeth:

COCA: *People smile all the while.*
Lots of zip and lots of style
On the street of dreams,
Ninety-seventh Street!

Neon signs light the sky.
Foghorns croon a lullaby
On the street of dreams,
Ninety-seventh Street!

Another variation on the standard movie musical involved the unknown who becomes a glittering star while her husband, also a star, falls into disrepute and oblivion. The best-known version of this basic plot is *A Star Is Born*, filmed in 1937 with Janet Gaynor and Fredric March, in 1954 with Judy Garland and James Mason, and in 1976 with Barbra Streisand and Kris Kristofferson. On two of these three occasions, young Esther Blodgett was transformed into movie luminary Vicki Lester, while her husband plummeted to failure and suicide. It was a serviceable story line, but ripe for satire.

"Your Show of Shows" plucked the fruit from the vine with "Star Struck." Here, Imogene Coca begins as an old lady telling her granddaughter the story of how she became a star and also the wife of Rod Rodney (Sid Caesar), a movie star in his own right. In a flash-

back, we see Rod at Baldwin's Chinese Theatre in Hollywood as the main attraction of a gala event: he is being immortalized in cement. Announcer Howie Morris informs us that "right next to the immortal paw prints of Rin Tin Tin, the knee prints of Marlene Marlene, and the famous profile of Barry Barrington," the world will now have the imprint of Rod Rodney's world-famous widow's peak. With the unswerving logic of the insane, several men turn Rod upside down and stick his head in the cement! Tons of coins fall from his coat pockets.

Enter Coca in shabby coat and beret, a wistful autograph-seeker with pencil and paper. Wandering onto the set of Rod's newest movie, she appears at an opportune moment: leading lady Judy Johnson is inadequate, and Rod Rodney is furious. "Anybody in the world could do this part better than she can!" he roars. And who is the lucky "anybody" who gets her big chance? Right.

Against director Carl Reiner's wishes ("A little girl off the street? An autograph hound?"), Rod insists that she play the scene with him:

COCA: *Me? Play a scene with Rod Rodney?*

CAESAR: *Yes! You can do it!*

She continues to protest but he gives her the lead-in lines, and suddenly, as everyone watches in stunned admiration, Coca gives a full professional reading:

COCA: *I should have known it long ago. It was silly to pretend it could be any other way. [Turns away] I was living in a dream world. [Walks to window] What right did I have to think I could achieve happiness! [Her voice rises] Happiness is reserved for people who were born on the right side of the tracks! Love is only for those who can afford it! The rest of us have to forget about love! [Turns on him] I hope you'll be very happy, Hartford. I hope your conscience* will never bother you when you remember that you robbed a woman of her laughter and left her alone and desolate in a world that is empty and meaningless. [*She bursts into violent sobs.*]

CAESAR: [*Recovering*] You see? I told you an idiot could play this part. And we found the idiot!

Naturally, she gets the part. Naturally, she and Rod fall in love and marry. And naturally, she is renamed Mary Sweet. In only a few months, she is a top-ranking star with a husband slipping into oblivion. In a familiar movie device for advancing the plot, the headlines tell the story: NEW STAR IN FILMS. MARY SWEET OUTSHINES HUBBY. RODNEY OPTION DROPPED BY MIRACLE FILMS. AMERICA'S SWEETHEART COPS ACADEMY AWARD.

At the Academy Awards ceremony, Mary is grateful but glum without Rod beside her. "I love Rodney," she tells her director. "Success is nothing without him." "Mary, you're just . . . too good!" he says, perhaps echoing the sentiment of every Esther Blodgett watcher over the years. She accepts the Oscar with an appropriately humble speech:

COCA: *I must be dreaming. I don't believe it's true. . . . Ever since I came to Hollywood, it's been like a dream. I hope I never wake up because it's a wonderful dream. But I don't really deserve this award. It should go to the man who made all this possible . . . Thomas Edison!*

Enter Rod Rodney, plastered. In the venerable *Star Is Born* tradition, he staggers to the microphone and harangues the audience:

CAESAR: [*Throwing the Oscar on the floor*] One day they give you statues, the next day they throw mud in your face! The public! The great public! You forget pretty fast, don't you? Remember me? I was America's sweetheart. Me! Ron . . . Phoney!

He swings his arms and accidentally hits Mary in the mouth, knocking out a few teeth. ("It's all right, darling," she reassures him. "They were only caps.")

Later, in the park, Rod staggers in, a pitiable wreck bemoaning his fate. Once Mary was a little nobody and he was a big man. Now *he's* a little nobody, and *she's* a big man. There is only one way out: suicide. ("It's time for the grand exit.") He tries to kill himself—but fails even at that. He attempts to shoot himself in the head, but misses, shoots a second time and misses, tries a third time—and misses again. "I'll get myself yet!" he insists. Once more he shoots and misses! His grim determination, coupled with his abysmal aim, make for one of the comedian's finest moments on "Your Show of Shows."

When we come back to aged Mary Sweet, née Stumbler, who sends her granddaughter off to bed, we learn that, unlike the hero of the film versions, Rod Rodney has survived. He and Mary settle down to watch one of their old movies on television.

Other familiar movie genres were spoofed with refreshing regularity on "Your Show of Shows." In "Emergency," the "Men in White" hospital drama, complete with dedicated surgeon, crusty old hospital superintendent, his flighty daughter, and a mysteriously ill girl from nowhere, was deftly satirized.

Caesar, of course, is the surgeon, a relentlessly noble sort with a "radical" theory of physiology. "I believe that somewhere in the body there is a place for the brain," he tells the superintendent (Carl Reiner). "I don't know where but I'm sure there is." Dr. Hamilton adheres faithfully to the Hippocratic Oath, even when he's not exactly sure what it is:

CAESAR: [*With stirring music behind him*] When I took that Hippocritical oath, I didn't take it as a hypocrite— others may be hypocrites about the Hippocritical oath but if hypocrites meant that hypocritically speaking, sir, I'm hip and no hypocrite is going to tell me—and I'm also hip to a lot of things that go on around here.

The superintendent's daughter Nancy (film actress Pat Crowley) breezes in, chattering about yachts and lunch at the Snob Club, but Dr. Hamilton is not interested, especially when he hears about a mysterious new patient. A girl has been admitted who doesn't remember her name or address. She is in a dazed condition, has two rings on her left hand, rhinestone earrings, and shoelaces untied on her right shoe. In case that isn't sufficiently baffling, she is also suffering from a nosebleed. The doctor is elated: here is a chance to work at last on a clear case of "cycloramic amnesia!" Nancy storms off in a fury, fed up with her fiancé's all-consuming dedication to duty.

A closeup of Imogene Coca's crossed eyes, and we learn that she is the patient with amnesia, distraught at her condition. "What was the last thing you remember before you blacked out?" an intern asks her. "Everything went white," she replies. She strives mightily to remember something—anything—but all she can come up with is a dog food commercial: "Nippy Dog Food tastes so great/ Makes your puppy glad he ate/ Full of precious vitamins/ Look for Nippy in the big red tins. I like Nippy. Woof, woof, woof." Now on the case, Dr. Hamilton tries a word association test with Coca:

CAESAR: *Bread.*

COCA: *Butter* [They continue in this vein, then:]

CAESAR: *Hickory*

COCA: *Dickory*

CAESAR: *Dock.*

COCA: *The mouse*

CAESAR: *Ran up*

COCA: *The clock.*

CAESAR: *The clock. The clock . . .*

COCA: *The clock.*

CAESAR: *The clock.*

COCA: *The clock.*

CAESAR: [*Intensely, onto a lead*] *The clock. What about the clock?*

COCA: [*Very pleased with herself*] *The clock struck one and down he run. Hickory dickory dock! Hurray!*

The good doctor is determined to find a cure. When he calls the superintendent an idiot, an old fogey, and a stick-in-the-mud for refusing to let him continue his experiments, Reiner strips him of his medical rank. Like an officer humiliating a court-martialed soldier, he removes Caesar's stethoscope and prescription pad, and breaks his tongue depressor in two. "You've depressed your last tongue," he tells an unrepentant Caesar.

With Howie Morris as his loyal assistant, Caesar goes on with his experiments with Coca. His instructions are replete with medical mumbo jumbo:

CAESAR: *The first phase is to prepare the patient with an injection of twenty cc's of siliohelium. And ninety-eight cc's of mindymycin. . . . And then we apply my memory pusher to the arm of the patient and exert pressure of tremendous force so that the mind is pushed from the subconscious into the conscious. But we have to be very careful. . . . If we apply too much pressure, she might blow her top.*

Pausing only to inject his own finger by mistake (another splendid Caesar reaction to pain), the doctor moves to the crucial moment of the experiment. On the theory that when a patient is drowning, his whole life flashes before his eyes, Caesar has Coca lowered into a tank nearly filled with water. On the first try, she comes up gasping for air. "I remember, I remember!" she cries. "Who are you?" Sid asks, success close at hand. "Esther Williams!" she replies. On a second try, she is under the impression she is Johnny Weissmuller. On the third try, success:

125

COCA: *My name is Hilda Frankenheimer, and I live at 226 Canal Street, and I'm employed at the Chi Chi Hat Company in Paterson, New Jersey.*

CAESAR: *[Going to Coca] Thanks for your faith in me.*

COCA: *[Spritzing Caesar with a mouthful of water] And thanks for the memory! [They embrace.]*

Another popular movie genre given the satirical treatment on "Your Show of Shows" was the prison melodrama. Any movie buff who had ever seen James Cagney, George Raft, or John Garfield as the kingpin convict in a simplistic view of prison life, courtesy of the brothers Warner, would immediately recognize the situation in "Prison Walls." Sid Caesar plays Big Mike, tough, deadly, ruthless, and not terribly bright. Coming out of solitary, he offers the benefit of his experience to fellow inmates Carl Reiner and Howie Morris:

CAESAR: *While I was in solitary, I spent a lotta time thinkin'. I did a lot of thinkin'! I got a lot of thought ... I thought about the walls ... the bars ... the guards with the guns. You know what I figured out?*

REINER: *What?*

CAESAR: *We're in prison.*

Visited by his loyal girlfriend (not Ann Sheridan but Maria Riva, Marlene Dietrich's daughter), he tries to kiss her through the mesh screen between them, but fails. ("I've got to get a girl with longer lips," he thinks.) The girl reminds him of his promise: "Remember when they were taking you away? Remember what you said to me? You said ... don't worry, baby, they haven't built a prison that can keep me away from you!" "They built it!" Big Mike tells her. "This is it!"

Nevertheless, in keeping with movie tradition, he is prepared to break out that evening, and he sets up his plan. Unfortunately, he fails to account for the rampant stupidity of his fellow conspira-

tors—they garble the whispered messages from cell to cell, and when they break loose, they bump into each other in their panic. Big Mike is justifiably furious: "What's the matter with you fellas? Didn't you ever do a prison break before?"

Finally in a time-honored scene, Big Mike is alone, trying frantically to climb over the wall while his girl and the warden plead with him to surrender. As he leaps at the wall, a spotlight hits him and for one fleeting moment, he becomes George Jessel in stripes, paying a musical tribute to his mother:

CAESAR: *[Singing] One bright and shining light, that taught me wrong from right ...*

The warden tells him that if he cooperates, he might get a break after all, but Big Mike is dubious:

CAESAR: *Yeah. Nobody ever gave me a break. I never had a break in my whole life. When I was a kid, I never had things like the other kids had. I never even had an orange. [They throw him an orange] Now you give me an orange. I never had a decent meal to eat. [They throw him a sandwich; he opens it] I never had no mustard! [They throw him mustard] I never had a gun ... a thirty-eight ... a forty-five ... anything. [He waits a minute] Cheapskate.*

But all ends well when Big Mike gets a last-minute pardon and proves his innocence, all in sixty seconds.

In "Three-Star Semi-Final," "Your Show of Shows" took on the newspaper melodrama. As in *His Girl Friday* and scores of lesser imitations, here was the ace reporter (appropriately named "Ace" Johnson), battling for exclusive stories and headlines with a live-wire lady reporter he actually loves. His essential battered hat in place on his head (with the brim up, of course), "Ace" comes hurtling into the newspaper office: "Stop the press, children, headline! 'Ace'

"The Slums of New York": Bad Mike (Sid Caesar) and his hoods menace his brother Allan (Carl Reiner) as Rosie (Imogene Coca) looks on.

Johnson scoops again! I got a story that will stand this town on its ear!"

In comes Coca as Sally the Sob Sister. Wearing the requisite tailored suit and horn-rimmed glasses, Sally is angry with "Ace" for standing her up on their date. He distracts her with a hot story tip: "There's gonna be some action at the Club Hi Ho tonight. Somebody's gonna get bumped off!"

COCA: [Sardonically] You've got printer's ink in your veins.

CAESAR: So that's what makes me nauseous all the time.

COCA: [Decides to give him one more chance, takes off her glasses]

CAESAR: Sally! I've never seen you without your glasses. [Pause] Put them back on!

Later, Sid turns up at Club Hi Ho, where he is warned by top hood Carl Reiner to stay away. The stage show begins, and out trots the line of chorus girls, containing one conspicuous member: Sally the Sob Sister, still wearing her glasses. A torchy girl singer comes out on the floor.

SINGER: [With full-throated emotion] I'm gonna live till I die! [A shot rings out,

and she falls dead. General pandemonium.]

Now Sally reappears, all excited. She has taken a picture of the murderer with her camera!

COCA: The proof is right in this camera! I know who killed the girl!

REINER: [Making a threatening gesture] Who was it?

COCA: [Turning from him to an innocent bystander] It was you! [Turning to Sid] It was him! [Turning again] It was . . .

Carl and his hoods hold them all under the gun, but eventually fearless "Ace" Johnson takes charge and subdues the gang. The sketch closes with him calling the story in to the newspaper, an adoring Sally beside him.

One of the best of the movie satires was a send-up of the "New York" movie in which two brothers, backed by the loyal girl from their childhood, set out to "conquer" the city but head in opposite directions. (The prototype was the 1934 movie, *Manhattan Melodrama*, with Clark Gable, Myrna Loy, and William Powell.) In the "Show of Shows" version, called "The Slums of New York," Caesar played Mike, softhearted roughneck who turns crooked. Carl Reiner was Allan, his bookish brother who becomes district attorney, and Coca played Rosie, the girl loved by both of them.

In the New York setting ("city of hope and despair, city of a million success stories and a million failures," an offstage announcer tells us), Allan is already on his way to being the best-read boy in the neighborhood. Rosie admires him ("Someday, you'll be very famous and very nearsighted"), but she has a yen for Mike:

COCA: [Transported] I'll tell you what Mike means to me. [Max Steiner-like music] Mike has something about him. A quality. He's full of life. He's vibrant. He's adventurous. He's romantic. He's exciting.

Mike is also in trouble, with the cops in pursuit. But he's determined to be a "father" to Allan, just as he had promised:

CAESAR: I promised Poppa when I told him I'd be the head of the family to make something out of you, and I'm gonna keep that promise. Someday, somewhere, somehow, sometime, someplace, you're gonna be a big lawyer. The biggest lawyer this city ever saw, and someday, somewhere, somehow, sometime, someplace, you're gonna get me out of jail. Show me how smart you are. Spell something for me.

Allan spells "magnanimous," making Mike deliriously happy, so happy that he plans to steal a chicken for him the next night. "Now go home and study," he tells him. Rosie, in the meantime, is torn between the two brothers. "Why can't Mike be like Allan," she moans, "and Allan be like Mike?"

The years pass, and not unexpectedly, Mike is Public Enemy No. 1, and Allan, now an important lawyer, is planning to run for district attorney. Inevitably, a rift develops between the two, with Allan refusing to have anything to do with his criminal brother. ("We're on different sides of the fence and that's how it's going to be from now on!") Rosie is distraught:

COCA: Allan! He's your brother! Your own flesh and blood! How can you talk to him like that? He raised you. He fed you when you were a little baby.

The brothers fight and separate, but not before poor Rosie gets between them and loses a few teeth in the process. Clearly, however, she still has this "feeling" for Mike.

In the climax, Rosie is kidnapped by Mike's henchmen and taken to his penthouse apartment. Mike will use her as bait to lure Allan to their old neighborhood and kill him. The confrontation comes at the stoop of their old brownstone. Nobly, Mike tries to warn Allan that he's in danger, but Allan refuses to leave. Instead, he gives Mike one last chance to run before being arrested.

CAESAR: For Poppa's sake, you run!
REINER: For Momma's sake, you run!
COCA: For heaven's sake, let's all run!

When henchman Howie Morris tries to shoot Allan, Mike leaps between them and gets the bullet. He confesses to a certain surprise: "I don't understand it— he was always such a lousy shot, that Slimey." As he lies dying, he asks for one final favor from his brother.

CAESAR: Spell something for me.
CARL: [Crying] Magnanimous. M-a-g-n-a-n-i-m-o-u-s.
CAESAR: Thanks, Allan. Poppa would have been proud. [He falls back, then gets up again] . . . Rosie, I want you to marry Allan 'cause he's good for you . . . [The end title flashes on the screen but he gets up again] . . . Allan, I want you to marry Rosie. She'll make you a good wife! [He tries to get up again, but Rosie pushes him down for good.]

COCA: *It had to end like this!*

Now the end title flashes on the screen—and *stays* there.

Occasionally, one of the program's film satires would combine several familiar plot lines. In "I'm in Love," the writers blended the erudite-professor-ruined-by-cheap-girl story of *The Blue Angel* with the man-of-quality-obsessed-with-sluttish-waitress story of *Of Human Bondage*. The result was another splendid spoof.

Sid is Professor Ludwig von Brenner, eminent German scientist, who arrives in England to address the British Academy on his new theory of psycho-brain therapy. His theory is worth quoting:

CAESAR: *My theory about the brain is that the brain is bigger than the mind. The brain is everything. The whole shooting match. But the mind is nothing. You want to cross your legs you need the brain. The mind can't make up its mind. And the heart is just a pump and the liver is just for laughs. The brain is everything.*

In a diner with his closest friend Peter (Carl Reiner), the Professor meets Ivy (Coca), a tawdry and grasping waitress, who bowls him over completely. "I feel a strange feeling," he says. "A wonderful feeling, I feel. I never had a feeling like this before." Immediately, he offers to give her everything she wants. A new hat, new stockings, and money for her mother's operation. "Maybe you have a kid brother who would like to go to camp?" he asks her.

Shockingly, Professor von Brenner has fallen in love with a woman Peter refers to as "a frowsy frumpy flossie." Weeks later, shabbily dressed, in a tacky hotel room, the Professor can think only of Ivy. He receives a call from Heidelburg (rendered in double-talk by Howie Morris) that he is now "raus, gespelled, gefired" from his position at the uni-

versity. Peter tries desperately to help—"one of the greatest minds of our time is just melting away"—but the Professor refuses to listen. Ivy is "sweet," and he is "the luckiest man in the world." Inwardly, however, he knows that he's ruined his career.

Enter Ivy, now dressed in "snazzy" fashion but no less nasty or ungrateful. The Professor proposes to her, and she gives him a dirty laugh and spits at him. "You didn't answer my question," he tells her. Ivy is insatiable: she wants everything, even his most prized possession, the gold medal awarded him by the university, a "first prize for smartness." He realizes now that she is nothing but a "gelt digger." Alone and desolate, he looks at the chandelier, gets a rope, stands on a chair, ties the rope to the chandelier—and pulls the chandelier down! "I ought to be able to get a couple of bucks for this," he says.

The Professor is now in the very dregs, working as a bus boy in Ivy's diner. But then Peter comes to tell him that the Academy still wants him to speak as the guest of honor at the annual banquet. Summoning up his last resources, the Professor attends the banquet—with Ivy brazenly on his arm. As he addresses the august company, Ivy insists on having her cigarette lighted. Shakily, the Professor complies, and as she blows smoke in his face, he begins to come apart at the seams:

CAESAR: *I say: Don't listen to the heart. [Coca blows smoke in his face] The heart is no good. [Coca blows smoke again] Yes, ladies and gentlemen. This proves what I was saying. Listen to the brain, not to the heart. [Picks up the knife] My heart tells me to stab her right in the back. My brain says no, in the front. [Stabs her, she dies] You should only listen to your brain up here because you don't need a heart. The heart is nothing. [Stabs himself accidentally] What did I do here? Excuse me, ladies* and gentlemen. *I have to die.* [Dies.]

A final card reads: "A brilliant mind. But a foolish heart."

Inevitably, a prime target for the writers' freewheeling satire was not only the hallowed classic or genre that had made its way into the Movie Hall of Fame. There was also the contemporary film that topped the "Ten Best" lists of the critics, the prestigious movie that won—or would soon contend for—all the major awards. Weighed down with star power, a "name" director, expensive production values, and an extravagant publicity campaign, this type of film inspired literate analyses by the more articulate film critics. It also inspired the "Show of Shows" writers to puncture its pretensions with some well-aimed satire.

"I'm in Love"

Professor Caesar is enraptured by the waitress Coca.

He becomes her devoted slave . . .

and reaches the depths of degradation.

"A Trolleycar Named Desire": a showdown between Bill and Magnolia.

Whereas the satires of the familiar movie genres were tempered with affection, the satires of contemporary films were somewhat more malicious. Although Lucille Kallen has said, "We really did have great affection for everything that we parodied," Mel Tolkin has admitted that they did bring a more wicked attitude to the contemporary movie satires. The writers, he noted, were very young, after all, and on top of the world, so it was not surprising that they would feel slightly superior to pretentious films that were being taken too seriously.

At any rate, the program's send-ups of these films were hilarious. It was not only the plots that were being spoofed; it was also the acting styles, the camera techniques, the look-how-marvelous-we-are smugness of Hollywood's attitude.

One of the most highly praised movies of the time, released in 1951, was the film version of Tennessee Williams' A *Streetcar Named Desire*. It had received four Academy Awards, the New York Film Critics Award, and scores of enthusiastic reviews for its exceptional acting by Vivien Leigh, Marlon Brando, Kim Hunter, and Karl Malden, and its expert direction by Elia Kazan. The audiences of 1951 had been stirred and possibly a little shocked by Williams' drama centering on the conflict between Blanche DuBois, a disintegrating, desperate ex-Southern belle, and her brutish brother-in-law, Stanley Kowalski. The final, powerful scene showed Blanche, now completely broken and out of her mind, being taken to an asylum.

Grim stuff indeed, but in the hands of the "Show of Shows" troupe, it became an uproarious send-up of Williams' florid style and melodramatic excesses. Now called A *Trolleycar Named Desire*, it had Sid Caesar as Stanley, here renamed Bill, the beer-swilling lout who intimidates and then battles with Imogene Coca, garishly made up as Magnolia, a belle so relentlessly Southern she makes Scarlett O'Hara look like Calamity Jane. (In the two performances of the sketch, Magnolia's sister Thelma was played by Betty Furness and Binnie Barnes.) Wearing a stylishly torn undershirt, Caesar takes Marlon Brando's famous characterization in the direction it was already heading: into the realm of comic exaggeration. "You're dirty and filthy and sloppy," his wife tells him. " 'Smatta with you?" he bellows. "That's the way I *always* look."

Enter Imogene as Magnolia, a moth-eaten fur piece draped around her shoulders. Lickety-split, Magnolia is off and running—at the mouth:

COCA: *Thelma, mah l'il ole sister, ah do declare! Mah, mah, mah! Ah thought ah nevah would get heah! That terrible ride on the terrible dusty ole train, an' when ah fahnally got here, ah had to wait hours for a streetcar! . . . So this is your little place! Mah, mah, mah!*

"What's with the mah, mah?" Bill asks, only to be studiously ignored by the chattering Magnolia. She is delighted to be at her sister's house—delighted to be *anywhere*, and plans to say "two or three years." Pressed to tell the story of her life in the past few years, Magnolia goes into a remarkable monologue that parodies Williams' Blanche DuBois just enough to be funny without lapsing into burlesque:

COCA: *Well, when ah left the plantation ah went to New Orleans, and there was a very rich gentleman who wanted to marry me. He kept buyin' me all kinds of diamonds and pearls, and he used to take me to the opera an' we mingled in high society, but ah just didn't love him enough to marry him, so ah got myself a position as a private secretary to this very wealthy gentleman who was madly in love with me. He belonged to the country club and he used to take me to all the lovely dances there an' he had a yacht and we used to go on moonlight cruises and he showered me with all kinds of beauti-*

ful gifts, but ah didn't love him enough to marry him, so ah decided to come heah and visit with. . . .

She is turned off only when sister Thelma shouts irrationally at her husband: "Shut up! Can't you see my sister's talking?" "I didn't say nothin'," says a baffled Bill, only to be called an "idiot" and a "moron" by Thelma.

The confrontation scene between Magnolia and Bill is the highlight of the sketch. As Bill munches his chicken sloppily, he eyes Magnolia, and not liking what he sees, he walks away from her. She follows him but remains at a good distance. Their eyes meet. A moment of hostile silence, and then:

COCA: *You take your hands off me! You get away from me, you beast! You get away from me, you heah? Don't you touch me! You take your hands off me! I'm used to being with gentlemen! I'm used to being treated like a lady!*

When Thelma accuses him of trying to attack Magnolia, he does the most sensible thing (it occurred to Stanley Kowalski but he never quite made up his mind to do it): he simply pushes Magnolia out of the door and out of their lives forever. No Southern gentleman, he.

The same year that Warner Brothers released *A Streetcar Named Desire*, Paramount was attracting sizable audiences with a film version of Theodore Dreiser's novel, *An American Tragedy*. Called *A Place in the Sun*, it contended with *Streetcar* for awards (both movies lost the Oscar to *An American in Paris*), earning acclaim for its unflinching story of an ambitious young man's journey to the electric chair, for its superb photography, and for the first-rate performances by Montgomery Clift, Elizabeth Taylor, and Shelley Winters. Most critics and moviegoers agreed that the strongest scene in the film was the one in which Clift, desperately in love with rich and beautiful Liz, tries to do away with his fiancée, plain and pregnant Shelley. He takes her rowing on the lake with the clear intention of drowning her, but she obliges him by standing up suddenly in the boat and toppling overboard. He is accused—and convicted—of murdering her, the thought being equated with the deed.

"Your Show of Shows" writers took this scene and turned it into "A Place at the Bottom of the Lake," a sketch in which Coca excelled as Mildred, the dim and irritating "nebbish" Caesar frantically tries to drown. (Chaplin tried to drown Martha Raye in *Monsieur Verdoux*, with no funnier results than here.) Imitating the Winters whine, Mildred drives her intended to a desperation only Caesar could express with such pain and intensity:

COCA: *Oh, you're so good to me, Montgomery! How could I ever have thought you were trying to get rid of me so you could marry that society girl just because she's beautiful and rich and gorgeous and wealthy.*

CAESAR: *Don't be silly. Why should I want to marry her just because she's beautiful and rich and gorgeous and wealthy and lovely and beautiful and rich . . . [He bursts into tears.]*

Out on the lake, handily equipped with knife, gun, and chain, Montgomery sets about his grim task of wiping out the repellent Mildred. But she drones on and on . . . and on . . . leaving Montgomery with only one device he can fall back on: the "voice-over" conscience familiar in so many movies. (In the sketch, the voice was read offstage by Carl Reiner.)

COCA: *When are we gonna get married, Montgomery? Let's get married today. Why can't we get married today, Montgomery? You'll see, Montgomery, it's going to be real nice. We'll have a nice apartment with real nice furniture and real nice carpets and real nice curtains*

"*A Place at the Bottom of the Lake*": Montgomery *tries to strangle Mildred . . . unsuccessfully.*

at the window.... Montgomery, *whatta you thinking?*

REINER: [On mike] *How did I ever get stuck with this dopey dame?*

CAESAR: *Nothing, Mildred, nothing.*

When she unwittingly paints for him a picture of domestic horror ("I'll bring your lunch pail to work every day and I'll phone you every hour... and I'll never let you out of my sight"), Montgomery (via Carl's offstage voice) de-cides: "I've *got* to kill this girl!" And he tries, oh, how he tries! Goaded by one too many "real nices" out of this wretched girl, he attempts to strangle her. The background music (a good imita-tion of the requisite movie music for such situations) blasts forth ominously as fran-tic Montgomery tries to squeeze the life out of his nonstop talking machine. Cae-sar runs the gamut of grimaces as he presses tighter and tighter, his arm around her neck—but to no avail. She keeps on talking through it all:

COCA: *While you're at work, I can keep busy. I'll knit you a pair of socks, and then after dinner we could go to a movie maybe, and you'll see, it'll be real nice and maybe later we'll move to a larger apartment and we'll have five or six kids. ... You'll see, Montgomery. It's gonna be real nice.... [She pushes him away] You're very affectionate, Montgomery....*

Dauntless, Montgomery tries to get her to change seats with him while the music continues to crash around them. Now desperate, he suggests a new tack—and gets a surprising answer:

CAESAR: *Look, Mildred, it's still early. Why don't we go somewhere else? You know what's interesting? The top of the Empire State Building. What a view! We could stand near the edge.*
COCA: *Oh, I don't like it up there. I fell off once.*

Finally, irrevocably beaten, Montgomery turns back to shore. "We'll get married," he tells Mildred. "And it'll be real nice, and we'll have a real nice apartment...."

No popular film genre was safe from the barbs of "Your Show of Shows." The late forties and early fifties had seen the rise of the so-called "adult" Western in which the hard-riding, gun-slinging, two-fisted cowboys of old had been replaced by tortured, complex, high-minded actors wearing cowboy suits. The situations in which they became involved often seemed to represent some larger, more "serious" theme; the symbolism was sometimes simplistic: white cowboy suit (good) vs. black cowboy suit (evil).

In a sketch called "Dark Noon," the writers on "Your Show of Shows" fired away at the nobler-than-thou hero of Stanley Kramer's 1952 production of *High Noon,* which Fred Zinnemann had directed to high praise from most critics and an Academy Award for Gary Cooper as the self-righteous sheriff Will Kane. Here Caesar played Slim, the beleaguered sheriff whose wife Mary Ellen (Coca)

fails to understand why he insists on standing alone against the killer coming in on the next train. "Nobody's gonna help you, Slim," she tells him. "You won't get help from anybody." But Slim refuses to leave, waxing (or at least trying to wax) eloquent about his reasons:

CAESAR: *When a man flies outa the cage and the cayotes howlin' in the tumbleweed, when a horse can't rightly cross the bridge, when a cow is, that is, a man oughta if the moon is high in the cactus and ... when a coyote is chompin' in the corral ... when a jackrabbit can't ... unless there's a ... [to Coca] You better go. You'll miss the train, Mary Ellen.*

This failed attempt at lyricism is followed by a more reasonable assessment of his situation:

COCA: *[Furious] I can't understand it! How can you stay here and wait for a man to come and kill you?*
CAESAR: *'Cause I'm stupid, Mary Ellen.*

His only friend is Howie Morris, playing the eternal Walter Brennan-type who could always be counted on to support a foolhardy act. He pleads with the townspeople to help the sheriff:

MORRIS: *Before he became the sheriff, this town was a wild, lawless town full of drinking, gambling, and shooting. Since he's been the sheriff, it's different! [Shouts of "Yeah!"] He closed down the saloon, he cut out the gambling, he stopped the drinking!*
TOWNSMEN: *[As one] Kill the sheriff!*

As the fatal hour approaches, in a sly imitation of the source material, we see a montage of clocks and more clocks, ticking away the minutes to the confrontation of sheriff and killer. Bride Mary Ellen exhorts the cowardly townspeople, then comes to an inevitable conclusion:

COCA: *Look at him! He's willing to stay here and face the killer singlehanded! He's ready to give up his life! He's not* afraid to die! He don't mind if he ends up with a bullet in his head! He wants to die! He wants to lie there in the gutter! He knows he hasn't a chance! He knows they'll shoot him down like a dog! But he doesn't care. He's an idiot! And I'm getting out of town before it's too late.

Having exposed the foolishness of Slim's noble instincts, Mary Ellen pauses only to shoot the killer (Carl Reiner) before her husband can fire a shot. (In the confrontation scene, Sid and Carl take the famous long, slow walk toward each other to the ballad "You're Gonna Die," wailed by an offstage singer. Carl takes off his gun belt and throws it away. When Sid removes *his* gun belt, his pants fall down, and his strong, stony face suddenly crumples in tears.)

Another extremely successful "adult" Western of the period was *Shane* (1953), with Alan Ladd as the enigmatic, peace-seeking gunfighter who defends a group of homesteaders against a marauding cattle baron and hired henchmen. The brave exploits of Shane were seen through the eyes of an adoring boy, played by young Brandon de Wilde. The image of Shane, all in white on his white steed, was set against the image of mean Jack Palance, dressed in black astride his black horse.

Out of the West, by way of "Your Show of Shows," came "Strange," embodied by that stalwart defender of the downtrodden, Sid Caesar. He appears at the farm owned by Higgins (Howie Morris), where he attracts the worshipful attention of Higgins' son, played by Imogene Coca. They watch in awe as the stranger consumes buckets of water.

MORRIS: You seem mighty thirsty, stranger. Have a long, dry ride?
CAESAR: No, had a herring for breakfast!
MORRIS: What's your name?
CAESAR: Folks call me . . . Strange.
MORRIS: Strange? What's your first name?

CAESAR: Very. But you can call me Strange.
COCA: [Who has been admiring him] Gee, that's a nice gun, Strange. That's a nice holster, Strange. Nice gun belt, Strange. I like you, Strange. You got nice boots, Strange. You're nice, Strange.

Strange (or, if you will, Very) takes a dim and very un-Alan Ladd-like view of this nosey kid: "Get away, kid," he says, "or I'll blast you!"

Of course Strange has a change of heart when he sees how the Higgins family is being abused by gunslinger Barton (Carl Reiner, a devilishly natty figure in black). He decides to stay and help them, and his reason, characteristically blunt and to the point, sums up the entire Western genre:

MORRIS: Why are you staying here? You hardly know us. Why are you risking your life for us?
CAESAR: [Very brave] Cuz they're the bad guys and I'm the good guys. That's why.

Strange goes to town to buy a hundred pounds of flour for the family, and a lemon-and-lime lollipop for the boy. In Gaffer's General Store and Saloon, he discovers Barton and his men, itching for a fight. He has the "guts" to order a lemon-and-lime lollipop, and the following exchange ensues, a funny spoof of the infinite number of good vs. evil clashes in Westerns:

REINER: You know what you are? A lemon-and-lime lollipop-lickin' sodbuster.
CAESAR: [His cheek quivering] Did you call me a lemon-and-lime lollipop-lickin' sodbuster?
REINER: And not only that, you're a lily-livered lemon-and-lime lollipop-lickin' sodbuster!
CAESAR: Did you call me a lily-livered lemon-and-lime lollipop-lickin' sodbuster?
REINER: You're a low-down, lip-eared, lily-livered lemon-and-lime lollipop-lickin' sodbuster!

"Strange," a satire of Shane: *Virginia Curtis, Howie Morris, Sid Caesar, and Imogene Coca.*

CAESAR: [*Thoroughly confused*] Are you calling me a lily lowie lolly limey lemon eared . . . are you calling me a coward?

REINER: Yeah. [*He throws whiskey into Caesar's face. Caesar licks the whiskey from his lips. He continues looking at Reiner ominously. Then Caesar hiccoughs.*]

CAESAR: *Barton, don't push me too hard.*

But Barton does—and Strange finds himself in tears at the pain. ("All right, you did it. This is the first time in my life I cried and you did it!") His weakness is seen by the boy, who accuses him of being a coward. Humiliated, Strange draws himself up to full height—and throws whiskey in the boy's face.

Later, facing the villain in the general store, Strange discovers one small oversight: he forgot his gun. ("Oh, boy . . . no gun. That's a crazy thing. Didn't bring a gun to the gun fight.") But the boy tosses a gun to Strange, who proceeds to shoot all six of Barton's henchmen.

REINER: *Six shots. Six bullets. You're empty.*

138

[CAESAR *shoots and Reiner falls, with an incredulous look on his face.*]

CAESAR: *The only seven shooter in the West. Made it myself.*

Proud of his idol once again, the boy babbles away without letup:

COCA: *You did it, Strange. You got him, Strange. You killed him, Strange. You're a hero, Strange. You're a nice man. Strange. I like you, Strange.*

CAESAR: *Wish I had an eight-shooter.*

Strange goes on his cryptic way as the boy calls after him: "Come back, Strange. Strange, come back ... Strange [echo] ... Strange [echo] ... Strange [echo] ..." The last words are Strange's, echoing back to the boy: "Shut up, you rotten kid [echo] ... rotten kid [echo] ... rotten kid [echo] ... rotten kid ..."

Still another variation on the Western drama, "Tall, Dark, and Strange," turned up on another program. Here Sid Caesar played a heroic cowpoke who saves the town newspaper editor (Howie Morris) and his granddaughter Mary Jane (Coca) from the evil Black Bart (Carl Reiner). He first appears at the window of their house, lighting a cigarette. ("Just wanna keep my nose warm. Don't smoke but I like a warm nose.")

The Stranger, of course, knows no fear. He gets Black Bart to apologize—and even curtsy—for bumping into him. ("Don't you say excuse me when you bump into a tall, dark, handsome stranger?"), and he manages to shoot three of Bart's men with a single bullet. ("That was my famous three-in-one richochet bullet.") Naturally, Mary Jane is impressed: "They'll name a street in town after you. I can see it now. The Tall Dark Handsome Stranger Avenue." She begins to feel more than admiration, though the stranger, in his inimitable way, warns her: "Keep your claws off my heart."

When the Stranger is thrown into jail on a trumped-up charge, Mary Jane brings

him a cake, but—surprise!—it's only a cake, since she wouldn't do "nothin' illegal." Help comes from his faithful (and obviously intellectually superior) horse, who succeeds in tying a rope to the prison bars and pulling them down. The Stranger rushes out to save the day, still in handcuffs. At the editor's office, helpful Mary Jane tries to remove his handcuffs with a mallet, leading the Stranger to announce: "Be careful because I hate pain. If there's one thing that really hurts, it's pain. Nothing hurts me more than pain." She also tries to shoot them off, thoughtlessly aiming directly at his stomach until he suggests raising his hands above his head. In the end, the Stranger, still in handcuffs, manages to shoot Black Bart. "I believe you owe me two 'excuse me's,' " he tells Bart.

A short while later, editor Morris proudly displays his banner headline: "Mary Jane Marries Total Stranger."

On "Your Show of Shows," not only popular American movies were targets for satire. The wave of British films then attracting audiences to the box office did not go unnoticed by the writers. On two successive programs in March of 1953, the British movies *Breaking Through the Sound Barrier* and *The Seventh Veil* were satirized uproariously.

Released in the fall of 1952, the clumsily titled *Breaking Through the Sound Barrier* was concerned with a dedicated and obsessed builder of planes (Ralph Richardson) and his effort to construct a plane that will break through the sound barrier and extend the horizon of aeronautics. He is opposed by his daughter (Ann Todd), whose husband (Nigel Patrick) is a fearless pilot willing to test her father's experimental planes.

As interpreted by the "Show of Shows" writers, the movie, here called "Sneaking Through the Sound Barrier," became a parody of virtually every "test pilot" story conceived in either Hollywood or England. Carl Reiner is the determined inventor of the experimental plane, Imogene Coca his headstrong daughter Anne, and Sid Caesar the intrepid (and possibly feebleminded) test pilot Jim. When pilot Jim is told his new-fangled plane has no propeller (shades of Caesar's original plane routine!), he reacts with mild concern that turns swiftly into uncontrollable panic: "Not even a little propeller? Something to hold you up so you shouldn't fall down and hurt yourself?"

But he is soon back to his old brave self, staunchly reciting the Airman's Oath:

CAESAR: *I, as a member of the Airman's Association, do faithfully promise to keep my fusilage spick and span and never get fly specks on my goggles. I further promise that I will never throw out the garbage when I'm flying over a country and I will help old ladies across the continent. I touch my heart and hope to die, spit on three fingers, and look up at the sky.*

Jim keeps reassuring himself that he is "the most fearless daredevil in the sky, the greatest pilot in the world." But his fiancée is not impressed: "You'd rather tickle the stars than tickle me!" Not one to pass up the chance for a stirring speech, noble Jim expounds on his feelings about flying:

CAESAR: *You don't know what flying means to me. When I'm up there in my plane, above the clouds, and the earth is way down below me, and I can shake hands with the man in the moon. I get a feeling like I'm a part of all the open space around me and the blood sort of courses through my veins and rushes wildly to my head and my knee caps buckle and I have a funny feeling in my stomach like I'm going to explode and I get nauseous. But when you come out of it, you feel so good.*

"You've got gasoline in your veins," Anne tells him.

Finally, the Big Day when the plane will be tested arrives. Anne's father is elated: "If Jim Johnson succeeds this afternoon, tomorrow we'll be living in a different world!" Jim has a more immediate problem: his flying suit is baggy. And he has a hysterical fiancée on his hands. "Don't go!" she shrieks. "Don't go!" "I've got to," he replies quietly. "All right," she says, suddenly calm.

From the cockpit, Jim reports: "She's holding up fine. My tabs are trim and my aerlon is stable. Everything under control." But then he begins to shake: "Uh, oh. Something's wrong. She's beginning to vibrate! I'm losing control! The plane's shaking! It's falling apart!"

COCA: *Bail out, Jim! Bail out!*

CAESAR: *I can't bail out! I'm still on the ground! It's a bumpy runway! . . .*

But true to the tradition, Jim succeeds in getting the plane into the air—and even breaks through the sound barrier. Anne is reconciled as she gives him a cheerful salutation of "Contact!" when he returns in triumph.

The Seventh Veil, a film of older vintage, was the inspiration for one of the program's funniest movie satires. The movie had been released in 1946, during a vogue for psychiatric stories of troubled people whose deeply buried secrets were destroying their lives. *The Seventh Veil* portrayed a gifted pianist (Ann Todd) and her relationships with several men, particularly her tyrannical teacher and guardian (James Mason). After being driven to the point of suicide and in a state of complete collapse, she was brought to an understanding of her motives and inhibitions by a psychiatrist (Herbert Lom).

The movie was a natural for spoofing the rather simplistic psychiatric approach and florid romanticism of the forties. Caesar played Sir Thomas, crochety, overbearing, and obsessed with music: "I breathe music, I eat music, I sleep music! I hear music in the trees, in the wind! If it weren't for music, I'd go stark, raving mad!"

Appointed guardian to Pamela (Coca), he is determined to turn her into a brilliant concert pianist. Imitating James Mason's icy sadism in *The Seventh Veil*, he orders her to play, and when she refuses vehemently, he not only threatens her with his cane, but smashes the piano keys with it, an inch away from her delicate fingers:

CAESAR: *Let me see your hands. [He holds them] Yes, they're your mother's hands. The pinkies are in the right place. But the fingers are too short. The fingers must be longer. We'll have to stretch them. [Stretches her fingers with cracking sounds] One octave, two octaves, three octaves—there, now you're a four-octave girl.*

Now that she has the *hands* of a pianist, he proceeds to show her how she must develop the *heart* of a pianist—she must learn how to suffer. Practicing a glissando for her benefit, he hurts his thumb and grimaces in pain: "There, that's suffering. See the boo-boo?"

Pamela begins to practice incessantly—in a montage we see her playing while eating a sandwich, falling asleep at the keys, playing while brushing her teeth. Finally, she is ready: "You are a coiled spring, ready to be sprung," Sir Thomas tells her, whereupon Coca hops off to her room like an agitated yo-yo, to exaggerated sound effects. When a friend (Howie Morris) objects to his treatment of Pamela, Sir Thomas tells him: "Do you realize what I've done? I've taken a raw, ignorant girl and made her a talented nervous wreck! Tomorrow night she will play her first concert at Prince Edward Hall!"

But fate intercedes when Pamela, relaxing at a nightclub before her debut, meets American band leader Chuck Peters (Carl Reiner) and proceeds to fall madly in love with him, and he with her. When Pamela breaks the news to Sir Thomas, calmly telling him that she'll never play the piano again, he is totally enraged. (It is one of Caesar's most inspired moments: he waits a moment, allowing the dire news to sink in, then rises ever so slowly, shaking with anger until he is in the throes of a convulsion. He raises his cane to strike the ebullient Chuck Peters, crying: "I'll kill him!")

Pamela defies him at last, playing the piano with abandon as she speaks: "I'm not afraid of you any longer, Sir Thomas! I'm going to lead my own life! There are other things besides music! There's love and happiness! And I'm going to have them! I'm going to live! I'm going to be free!" But then Sir Thomas smashes the keys with his cane. Pamela stops, looks at him, and begins to play a Chopin waltz. When the friend accuses Sir Thomas of being in love with Pamela himself, he denies it as "preposterous," but in the next minute, he is down on his knees beside her, professing how he feels about her.

On a grueling tour, Pamela collapses completely, unable to cope with this "great maelstrom of indecision": whether to choose art and work—or love and happiness. Sir Thomas and Chuck Peters both plead to be chosen. Finally, after much brow-furrowing and heavy breathing, she decides on Chuck: on "Life. And Happiness. And music I can whistle." "Tough luck, old man," Chuck tells the desolate Sir Thomas. "Thanks for the piano lessons," says Pamela, perhaps a mite cruelly.

They leave, but a moment later, Pamela is back, to join Sir Thomas in a duet at the piano. She has chosen art and work after all.

"Your Show of Shows" also indulged in takeoffs on foreign films. Talented filmmakers from France, Italy, and Germany were establishing a strong reputation in this country, and films by Rossellini, De Sica, Renoir, Pagnol, and many others were widely attended in art theaters across the country. The producers and writers of "Your Show of Shows," though also appreciative, were not blind to the excesses of foreign films, and aided by a troup of performers, especially Caesar and Reiner, who were gifted at simulating foreign tongues, they began to turn out spoofs of the most familiar European movies.

A side note: Caesar has said that his ability to imitate foreign speech came from listening to the customers in his father's restaurant. In a May, 1972, article in *Esquire*, he demonstrated this ability briefly with speeches in mock-foreign tongues:

ITALIAN: *"Buon giorno signore e signore. Il fate luo lomani la menta cucelli tuo la lamana de la larote, mangiare! Mangiare supillia a de tuo pillente de la cosa cinque lara senta Madison Avenue. La rotara e la robanda esso lo vehiculo messo de lo typico de Bonnie's. Rutti de la gettina. Bonnie's e rolla in. Notta Bonnie's fua nu, ma Bonnie's fua mi. Ahma know Bonnie. Che lo mimaldo de lo trico e mimaldo della mangiare alatta, size of one to two!"*

FRENCH: *"Bonjour, messieurs et mesdames. Eh! Contrer d'Isabelle déja vu ballpenne répris à l'on très bien. Fetes toujeés marjoulles de lousondres, toute de suite cabibier that perdit la grand armée. Et elle pour le soldat avec le bayonet. Le bayonet, n'oublie pas, c'est sur son quelque on d'end of de rifle. Le bayonet rabit de façon very sharp. D'on use for ni de nails, or cut your hair. Strictly keep it en de case, unless I tell you to change. Then I will not be with you. Non?"*

GERMAN: *"Achtung! Was ist mir in die Harnuche eben wehler das ganza Romantic Hour. Das heer oder Hermann schlechte Romanz Das Durrementldorf das Lesson von kissen. Das lips von der ahnmal bereben aht dat Pucker. Pucker vith das lips! Pucker und weier denn mi von dan Puck, next to the vun dot you luff. Wenn der Puck kommt to der odder Puck, smack it away. Mit der schleck."* *

Italian movies, with their operatic emo-

* Reprinted with permission.

tions and often florid acting styles, were perhaps the most popular target. (The sight of Imogene Coca in her Anna Magnani fright wig is a cherished memory of many television viewers.) The characters were usually rough-and-ready peasants, concerned with the basic verities of life: birth, passion, marriage, death, and pasta. In "Bambino," a tot is left in a basket on the doorstep of a confirmed bachelor. In "The Cobbler's Daughter," the wayward girl of the title refuses to have anything to do with her father's foolish apprentice and has a clandestine affair with a dashing customer. "Presto!" has excited villagers Caesar and Coca winning a new automobile in a lottery.

In "Il Sono Mariago, or: Say You'll Be Mine," the entire situation revolves about Caesar's attempt to propose marriage to Coca, while her overanxious parents look on. Caesar is the shy and clumsy lout, unable even to give up his hat or the flowers he's brought to Coca when he comes to call. He sits with Coca and her parents on the sofa, trying to find a point at which he can propose marriage, but thwarted by the almost nose-to-nose presence of Mama and Papa. They finally leave but each time Caesar moves to embrace Coca, they return with heaping platters of food. (In one marvelous moment, Sid takes out a small ring box and removes, not an engagement ring, but a pill to quiet his nerves.)

Caesar manages to propose despite all the interference, Mama and Papa are overjoyed, and they all sit down to enjoy a hearty spaghetti supper. Mama warns Sid about his beloved's "hot" sauce, but he plunges ahead fearlessly, only to react violently at the first taste. In a series of perfectly timed moves, Caesar (a) indicates that he's on fire, (b) takes a sip of water, (c) has a cloud of hissing steam around his head, (d) wipes his mouth with his napkin, and (e) shows the huge hole burned in the napkin. Nevertheless, he proposes a toast to his impending marriage. They all drink, and once again Sid is "steaming," but happy.

It is a brief, unelaborate, but brilliantly handled sketch, in which the authentic-sounding Italian dialogue, fast, voluble, and fruity, is neatly complemented by the appearance of the actors, particularly Caesar with his plastered hair, ill-fitting suit, and nervous twitchings. Coca, as usual, uses her shy grin to great advantage.

Vittorio De Sica's *The Bicycle Thief*, released here in 1949, was a revered Italian film of an impoverished man who has his crucial bicycle stolen from him. On "Your Show of Shows," it was used as a springboard for a sketch, "La Bicycletta," which had Caesar and Coca as a peasant couple bent on ripping off friend Carl Reiner's shiny new bicycle. Here again, the excessive gesturing and melodramatic flourishes lightly twitted (but in no way mocked or demolished) the conventions of Italian cinema.

French movies, awash in wine and passion, were also regularly satirized on "Your Show of Shows." In all of these sketches, as evidenced by such titles as "Hate," "Le Grand Amour," and "I Love You Strongly," romantic emotion was the order of the day. One prominent example was "Au Revoir, Ma Cherie," repeated several times during the run of the program.

This was a triangular World War I drama, in which waif Coca (could anyone look more comically waiflike than Coca?) shares her favors, as they used to be called, with two ardent soldiers, Caesar and Reiner. She meets Caesar at a railroad station, where he is about to depart with the troops. They clutch each other feverishly, moaning "Madeleine!" and "Jean!" In a hilarious extension of the usual farewell scene, he asks for a lock of her hair, which she readily cuts for him. He then takes out a test tube

"Il Sono Mariago," or "Say You'll Be Mine": the suitors, Sid Caesar and Imogene Coca; Papa and Mama, Carl Reiner and Angela Castle.

LA BICYCLETTA *begins as Carl Reiner enters with his shiny new bicycle. He pauses to mop his brow on this hot Italian day.*

*Carl discovers old friend Sid Caesar
. . . and Sid Caesar discovers Carl's new bicycle.*

Sid blows the bicycle horn and is overcome with delight. He introduces Carl to sullen wife Imogene Coca. Imogene is not sullen for long, as she discovers Carl's bicycle. She is also overcome by the sound of the horn.

Sid and Imogene invite Carl to share a glass of wine.
Clumsy Carl spills some wine on his trousers and goes off to clean up . . .

. . . leaving Sid and Imogene to carry off the bicycle. Carl returns and prepares to mount his bicycle.

But he notices something is definitely wrong. Sid clearly has the same feeling.
Carl falls into despair at the loss of his bicycle—and goes off, a broken man. Sid and
Imogene are rhapsodic about their new acquisition. But Sid is suddenly remorseful,
remembering the good times with his old friend Carl.

He decides to return the bicycle, over Imogene's strenuous protests.
Carl, returning, is elated to have his bicycle back.

Remorseful, Carl confesses to taking some silverware while in their washroom.
But all is forgiven as the friends part. Imogene, however, has retained the bicycle horn,
and she grapples with Sid as the film ends.

and asks for a drop of her tears. Try as she may, she can't cry until Caesar pinches her. Sure enough, he catches a drop of her tears in the tube. They can barely part.

But as soon as he's left, in comes soldier Carl Reiner, and now the routine is "Madeleine!" and "Jacques!" They kiss, and this time his lips are stuck on hers, forcing him to pry them loose painfully. He makes love to Coca, and even gives her a wedding ring. When Caesar returns, Coca is unfazed. While both men profess their lifelong devotion (in lifelike French), she caresses their heads until they become aware of each other's presence. "Who is this man?" they each ask, and then both set upon Coca, berating her for her faithlessness. But suddenly, there is a call to arms and the soldiers

fall back into line. As the commander (Howie Morris) gives the order to march, women of the town rush on and, in the fashion made famous in *The Big Parade*, cling to the departing men's legs as they march off. Caesar, apparently not too overwrought at losing Coca, pauses briefly to pick up another girl and exit with her.

Other French movies dealt with people trapped in what a hard-breathing announcer might describe as webs of passion, deceit, and danger. In "Frère Jacques," a wounded French captain (Caesar), hiding from the Germans in World War I, takes refuge in a farmhouse where housewife Imogene Coca cheerfully hums the title tune as she removes the bullet from his leg. (This happens more than once, and she's cheerful every time.) In "The Sewers of

Paris," called "a warm, human love story, full of tenderness and beauty," ardent jewel thief Sid Caesar discovers that everyone—his girl Imogene Coca, his friend Carl Reiner, and even an old lady collecting money for charity—is a member of the police. In "I Love You Strongly or: I'll Be Seeing You," the characters are embroiled in intrigue in a cheap North African hotel, where, as a voice-over tells us, "shadowy figures of men and women on secret and dangerous missions move stealthily." ("The police are suspicious of everyone in this dim half-world of strangers.")

Love in a bakery was the subject of "Le Grand Amour." Here Coca was Michelline, a suicidal girl befriended by Louis the Baker (Caesar), who takes her home to his *pâtisserie*, where she'll be a pretzelbender. There she meets and falls instantly (but instantly) in love with Louis' assistant, Carl Reiner. She keeps retreating to a back room with Reiner, emerging each time with suspicious-looking white handprints on the back of her dress. At one point she returns with four handprints, prompting Louis to ask: "What's back there, an octopus?" Poor gullible Louis continues to accept her lame excuses (Reiner had to pick her up to reach the salt, or the chocolate for the chocolate pretzels), but finally he realizes the bitter truth and sends them both packing. Back at the dock where he rescued Michelline, another girl comes on in suicidal despair. She rants on about killing herself. With only a casual shrug, Louis pushes her into the water.

The more stolid, ornate, and somber movies out of German film studios were especially ripe for satire. Dumpling-heavy costume dramas and musicals were given their due, as in "Das Hertzig Glockenspiel or: My Beer is Your Beer," about a starving composer and his long-suffering frau, or "Ich Liebe Die Halls of Ivy," concerning nostalgic days in Old Heidelburg. The principals expertly imitated the harsh, gutteral sounds of the German language, and Howie Morris was a master at impersonating shrill, overbearing Teutonic types. In "The Grand Disillusion," a peculiar version of the Mata Hari story, he is the imperious Field Marshal, irritated by Caesar's willingness to answer spy Coca's strategic questions. "Was is gemacht here?" he asks Caesar. "Information, Please?"

Caesar is General Richenflichter, who comes to a cafe with his obsequious aide (Carl Reiner), where he spots Coca as she enters on the arm of Jack Russell. Enchanted by the alluring creature, he sends her a note, which she rejects huffily. Furious, General Caesar thrashes poor Reiner. When Coca tosses away the wine he sends her, the General is even more irate, and beats his aide even more severely. The next time, he sends her a bracelet, which she drops into her bosom, then razzes him arrogantly. Again, the aide is the hapless object of the General's terrible wrath.

Eventually, Caesar goes to her table, orders her escort to leave, and promptly plies her with champagne. Coca, of course, has other things in mind, such as the military secrets he's harboring. While he guzzles the champagne, she keeps tossing hers away to keep a clear head for business.

Enter Field Marshal Howie Morris, who expresses his irritation at the General's carelessness by putting out a cigarette in Caesar's hand. Doing a magnificent double take when he learns that Coca is the notorious Mata Hari, Caesar tries to get the information away from her, without success. In a final shootout, the Field Marshal and his men are all shot by Coca. She is aiming at Caesar when he begins to speak in French, removes his helmet, and puts on a dashing beret.

"Mata," says Sid. "Harry," says Imogene. And they embrace for a happy ending.

In "Ess Is Nicht Quiet Auf Der Vesten Front," a variation on the German war

Louis the Baker teaches Michelline how to make pretzels . . .

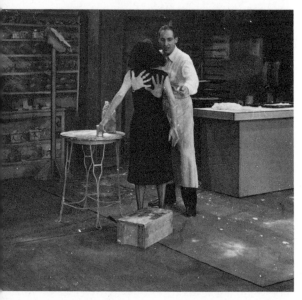

but she is more interested in Carl the other baker.

movie, the situation is reversed: this time Howie Morris is the obsequious aide to overbearing General Sid Caesar. He cleans the General's "ge-flyspecked" monocle, shines his shoes, and brushes his uniform. "Be careful when you're brushin' a Prussian," Caesar warns him. When the General inspects five of his soldiers, he harangues the last and sloppiest man, until Morris advises him that the soldier is the "Kaiser's kid." "How's Papa?" the suddenly affable General inquires.

In comes the sexy vamp (played by British actress Glynis Johns). When she insists on making love to General Caesar on the sofa, a frantic Morris keeps adjusting the General's uniform, fixing the creases in his trousers, reshining his shoes, etc. (He even smoothes the General's hair and eyebrows, carrying the German passion for order and neatness to the outer limits.) Enter Field Marshal Carl Reiner, who is shocked by Caesar's indiscretion and orders him court-martialed. Johns leaves, but not before eyeing Carl and muttering: "Und ein little spater mit du."

In a final scene of boundless hilarity, Caesar is stood before a firing squad after being stripped of his medals. (One medal, it turns out, is for the forty-yard dash!) Reiner is about to give the order to fire when Caesar requests a cigarette. Carl gives him a *very small* cigarette. Sid requests a king-size. Carl lights the cigarette, and Sid takes *very small* puffs, and even puts a toothpick in the cigarette. Carl knocks the cigarette out of Sid's hand and begins the order to fire. Sid requests one last word and begins chattering wildly. He stops, the order is given, and Sid begins chattering again. The situation is repeated, building in intensity until Sid himself gives the order to fire. Responding smartly and as one, the sol-

"Le Grand Amour," or
love in a French bakery.

diers shoot Carl, and Sid gives them all a five-day pass.

In "Die Grosste Shau in Der Welt," a *heavy* German drama of passion and violence in the circus, Caesar plays the Emil Jannings-like weight-lifter married to Coca, a flighty type with roving eyes. He accuses her of carrying on with the circus' high-wire walker, a slick type played by Carl Reiner. Coca denies it with a vehement "Nein, nein, nein." "Don't 'nein' me," he tells her in doggerel German. "I'm not a two-timer," she tells him, in equally imperfect German. "You shouldn't even be a one-timer," he claims.

When Coca leaves, Caesar gives his regular lesson in weight-lifting to Howie Morris. (Morris is not the best pupil—he keeps dropping the weights on Caesar's toes.) Meanwhile, Coca meets secretly with her lover, Reiner, who apparently walks on solid earth as if he were suspended on a wire high above the tent. He will take her away—they will do an act together for another circus ("Go dangle for the Dingling Brothers").

When Morris tells Caesar that his suspicions are true—wife Hilda *is* cheating on him with Reiner—Caesar falls into a rage and plots revenge. He sets up a heavy weight on a scaffold, arranging it so that it will come toppling down on Reiner's unsuspecting head. He invites Reiner to dinner and seats him directly under the weight. But when the moment of truth arrives, and he accuses Reiner of stealing his wife, his arrangement goes for naught: in a surprise gesture (not unfamiliar on "Your Show of Shows"), he simply pulls out a revolver and shoots Reiner. Coca tries to leave and he calls her back to have supper. He sets a place for her—plate, napkin, fork, spoon—and a knife, which he neatly plunges into her stomach. "The comedy is over!" he shouts. He hits the rope holding the scaffold—and the weight tumbles down on his head!

One of the funniest of the German

"Die Grosste Shau in der Welt."

film satires was "Der Prince Und Der Poppa," a "tragic" Graustarkian romance with a dollop of "La Bohème" added for good measure. Sid Caesar is dashing Crown Prince Rudolf, whose elderly father, the Kaiser (Carl Reiner), wants to prepare to take his place. (Papa, it appears, has a "bum ticker.") Caesar insists that he'd rather spend his time sowing wild oats, but his father assures him that his oats are "cooked." That night, at the grand ball, he must choose a wife.

At the ball, Sid is immediately smitten with Imogene Coca, a demure young thing with a faulty sense of direction. (He arranges to meet her at the beer garden, and she can't seem to remember how to get there. "Oh, yes," she finally recalls. "Right by Loew's Heidelburg.") Papa is visibly incensed by his son's choice, but Caesar is determined to court his lady love.

"Der Prince und der Poppa."

Prince Sid is smitten with Coca, but Poppa disapproves.

A *beer garden liaison* is interrupted, and the romance ends when Coca expires.

They meet at the beer garden (where Howie Morris is Caesar's effusive friend), and fall passionately into each other's arms. Enter an outraged Papa, who proceeds to rail at his son in a long speech that Carl Reiner makes a model of shrill Germanic gibberish. Then Papa turns to sentiment, reminding Caesar of all the things he did for him when he was a little boy (his "sailboat, choo-choo train, and pony"), causing Caesar to burst into a heartfelt chorus of "Oh, My Papa." They sob noisily on each other's shoulder. However, when Caesar insists that he still loves Coca, they quarrel. In a fury, Papa tears off Caesar's epaulettes, his medals, and finally—his moustache! He orders his guards to arrest his son and take him back to the palace.

Alone with Coca, the Kaiser asks her to give his son up—for the sake of the fatherland. Though anguished (a Coca-esque version of anguish, with comically distorted face and much wringing of the hands), she agrees to follow his wishes. The Kaiser, it appears, has a plan.

That evening, in the ballroom, Caesar is inconsolable at the sight of Coca surrounded by her admirers, laughing gaily and pretending he doesn't exist. When he goes to her, she spits at him and returns to her admirers as they drink champagne from her shoe. Obviously, this is Papa's ruse, designed to separate the lovers. Coca goes off to a corner to sob her little heart out, then starts to cough. In Camille fashion, she is stretched out on a chaise to expire, but not before she has confessed to Caesar that she really loves him. In despair, he realizes it has all been a trick. Conveniently, Papa has a stroke, and as he breathes his last, he tells his son that he is now the Kaiser. Solemnly, he gives Caesar his ring, his medallion, and, of course, his moustache. "Du bist Kaiser Rudolf," he murmurs, and dies. For the new Kaiser, this will undoubtedly be cold comfort on a winter night.

The satirical sketches on "Your Show of Shows" are unique in television annals. Seldom if ever tumbling into burlesque or knockabout slapstick, they offered wry and hilarious commentary on our foibles, attitudes, and cultural pretensions as expressed in our motion pictures. They also poked fun at acting styles and at hoary movie devices: abrupt closeups, bombastic music, and the like.

The sketches were also sophisticated in that they required the audience to bring a frame of reference to the material that was outside the usual home-and-family experiences. The creators of the program assumed that the viewers had a certain knowledge of films, both American and foreign, and that they would recognize—and laugh at—the clichés, the comfortable assumptions, and the occasional pomposity of these films.

They were right. And in making the film satires a regular feature of "Your Show of Shows," they gave the lie to those who felt that television comedy had to be simple and mindless because audiences have a limited attention span. The message was clear: witty, observant satire produced by formidable writing and acting talents could be successful on television.

A quarter of a century later, the message is still valid. Unfortunately, for most of this time, it has been ignored.

9

On Stage, Every-body!

"YOUR SHOW OF SHOWS" not only meant comedy and laughter; each week it also presented a selection of musical numbers that ranged from Tin Pan Alley to opera, numbers that showcased the versatile talents of the company's own singers and dancers as well as the exquisite skills of such legendary dancers as Alicia Markova and Frederic Franklin and such celebrated singers as Lily Pons and Jan Peerce. Few televised programs until that time (and few since) offered such an abundance of musical pleasures in a single program, and without gimmicks to make it more "palatable" to the average audience.

For most of the run of the show, there was a group of performers who appeared regularly, and whose faces became familiar to loyal viewers. In some cases, they were required to do double duty: dance as well as sing, or occasionally act in sketches or as the program's host or hostess. Most often, they provided tuneful and clever interludes to the show's comedy sketches and routines. They deserve to be remembered in these pages:

Bill Hayes and *Judy Johnson* were the program's resident popular singers, clean-cut, sweet-voiced, and appealing. They would perform solo, in tandem, or as lead singers in the show's musical production numbers. Bill Hayes, discovered by Max Liebman on a summer replacement television show with comics Olsen and Johnson (he had also appeared in their stage show, *Funzapoppin*), was featured in 121 editions of "Your Show of Shows." (Today, he and his wife Susan Seaforth are well known as the stars of the television soap opera, "Days of Our Lives.") Judy Johnson was a band singer with stage experience who joined "Your Show of Shows" in September, 1950.

Interviewed so many years later, Bill Hayes retains happy memories of his experience with "Your Show of Shows": "I worked with a marvelous, talented group of people. For me it was like going to school because I had very little background at that time.... Max Liebman was responsible for the magical rapport of everyone on the show. I applaud him ever since—every day—for getting that group together. They all worked together —fast, creatively, and well. Every show was timed right down to the second."

Recalling the perils of performing on a live show, Hayes had his share of nerve-shattering experiences. He remembers the time when he and Judy Johnson were singing "You're the Top," and the first trumpet player turned two pages instead of one and found himself playing fifty bars ahead of the rest of the orchestra. The orchestra was sputtering, and he and Judy were falling apart on stage. "We were desperately doing a time-step," he says. He also recalls the laughable (now, not then) incident in which, during a

Bill Hayes and Judy Johnson.

circle dance to the tune "I Miss My Swiss," he realized to his horror that he had forgotten to put elastic bands around the top of his leiderhausen and they were moving down around his ankles! ("I got mail about *that* for twenty years," he notes.)

Perhaps the most frightening incident occurred just before beginning a breezy rendition of "Any Place I Hang My Hat Is Home." Opera star Marguerite Piazza was introducing the number, and he was standing in the wings. "One of the stagehands knocked at some flats behind me—they were about forty feet tall. About six or seven of the flats slowly tottered and fell with a crash. If I had been standing about six or seven inches back, they would have made a grease spot out of me. They were that heavy. I walked out on stage with my heart beating wildly, and my first line in the song was 'Free and easy, that's my style.' "

The Billy Williams Quartette appeared in virtually all the shows, usually per-

forming two numbers in their jaunty, ingratiating style. The leader, Billy Williams, had formed the group years before, and it had achieved great popularity under the name of the Charioteers. The other members: Gene Nixon, Johnny Bell, and Claude Riddick.

Jack Russell, a singer with a strong voice, performed yeoman service on "Your Show of Shows" as the lead singer in many production numbers and as reliable support in operatic excerpts.

The Hamilton Trio. Made up of Bob Hamilton, Gloria Stevens (Mrs. Hamilton), and Pat Horn, this brilliant group danced its way through most of the shows. Chorus members in the musical *Inside U.S.A.* in 1949, they had formed their own dance trio shortly afterward. Appearing for one week as an after-season act at Tamiment, they were seen there by Max Liebman and signed for "Your Show of Shows."

Most of the numbers performed by the Hamilton Trio were "story" dances, in-

James Starbuck instructs singers Judy Johnson and Bill Hayes in their dance steps.

The Billy Williams Quartette.

Jack Russell.

ventively staged around a single incident or situation. In various sequences, they could be seen as: a private eye and his two comely suspects; a hunter and his prey, two scampering rabbits; jaunty calypso figures cavorting with their laundry on washday; a janitor and the disturbing figures in his dream; three raucous hillbillies; three office workers suffering from either the after hours or Monday morning blues, and even a lamp and two bookends!

Mata and Hari. Dancers of skill, subtlety, and boundless imagination, (Meta)

The Hamilton Trio.

Mata and Hari.

Mata and (Otto) Hari appeared for most of the program's run. Each of their segments combined dance and mime in harmonic proportions, with striking results. At various times, they could be seen as a bullfighter and his elusive prey; musicians at an orchestra rehearsal; rowdy, concertina-playing clowns; antic butterfly-chasers; marionettes with firm minds of their own, and inscrutable Indians performing their Fakir Dance.

Nelle Fisher and *Jerry Ross* were bright young dancers who began on the first show in February, 1950, and appeared almost every week until the eighty-sixth show on April 25, 1952. They danced their way blithely through many of the show's production numbers and in vigorous duets of their own.

Bambi Lynn and *Rod Alexander* succeeded Nelle Fisher and Jerry Ross, appearing first on September 6, 1952, in a dance to "Younger Than Springtime" that established their special lyrical quality. Some months later, they turned up again and remained to the end of the program's run. Gracefully gliding from one number to the other, these experi-enced dancers (Bambi Lynn had scored a triumph as Billy Bigelow's daughter in the original stage production of *Carousel*) were a particular pleasure to watch.

Marguerite Piazza appeared on the first show, and after singing gloriously for five months, she was finally signed by the Metropolitan Opera Company for a role in *Die Fledermaus*. While an opera star, she continued to sing on "Your Show of Shows," though not as regularly. Her arias and songs were a continually popular feature of the program.

Robert Merrill, one of the Metropolitan's distinguished singers, also appeared on the first edition of "Your Show of Shows" and left in March, 1951. He returned the following year for occasional guest spots.

"Your Show of Shows" also presented occasional special guests—leading popular singers such as Lena Horne, Pearl Bailey, and Nat "King" Cole, as well as cele-

Mata and Hari and company dancers in "Sports Newsreel."

Bambi Lynn and Rod Alexander.

Marguerite Piazza singing "Musetta's Waltz" from La Boheme.

Marguerite Piazza and Robert Merrill singing an excerpt from La Boheme.

Marguerite Piazza.

brated figures of ballet and opera, including dancers Alicia Markova, Tamara Toumanova, Maria Tallchief, Jacques d'Amboise, and Frederic Franklin, and opera stars Lily Pons, Patrice Munsel, Cesare Siepi, and Jan Peerce. Spotlighted with taste and style, these performers could be seen at their best on "Your Show of Shows." (They were never followed by jugglers or dog acts.)

Most of the closing segments of "Your Show of Shows" were elaborate production numbers that brought together the entire company of singers and dancers and often included the stars. Varying widely in approach and style, these numbers usually brought the proceedings to a exciting close. They were built around conceits of the Gay Nineties ("Bebe, the Belle of the Bowery," "The Hero, the Heroine, and the Mortgage Man," "The 8th Street Association Barbecue and

Lily Pons.

Fancy Dress Ball"). There were also numbers with a circus motif ("Here Come the Clowns"), a raffish "New York" approach ("The Lullaby of Broadway"), or a rah-rah collegiate style ("Oskiwowity University"). Some were full-scale excerpts from musical shows ("The Jazz Mikado") or self-contained mini-operettas ("A Night in Venice"). Occasionally, the closing segment would be a ballet staged around a popular story ("Tom Sawyer," with Coca as Tom), or a popular legend (James Starbuck as "Billy the Kid").

In many of the final production numbers Coca led the company in her inimitable rendition of a song from the past, such as "Glow Worm" or "Peaches Down in Georgia." The glow emanating from her extended to her fellow players, the studio audience, and the viewers at home.

These production numbers, and the people who performed them each week on "Your Show of Shows," were a vital part of the program. Perhaps their contribution can best be suggested by the photographs that appear in this chapter.

Lena Horne.

Nat "King" Cole.

Alicia Markova dances in an excerpt from Swan Lake.

Alicia Markova in "Dance of the Snowflakes."

Tamara Toumanova and James Starbuck.

James Starbuck in the "Billy the Kid" ballet.

"Sunday Morning on Wall Street."

The Currier and Ives production number.

10

Hail
and
Farewell

"YOUR SHOW OF SHOWS" ended its triumphant run on June 5, 1954, but the rumors about the demise of the program had started long before then. News items in early 1953 began to talk about the breakup of the show. Even earlier, there had been complaints that it was settling into too fixed a format, too similar a pattern. (In September, 1952, *Billboard* magazine wrote that the program "begins to show need of freshening. Despite its remarkable pace, it retains an air of familiarity.") The expertness and professionalism that had marked the show since its inception was being accepted as a fact and casually dismissed.

There were the inevitable stories about friction between the producer and the stars (untrue). There was talk about Sid Caesar wanting more money, or wanting his own show. The same was true for Imogene Coca, who was often depicted as weary of the weekly grind. An item in

the February 9, 1953, issue of the *Hollywood Reporter* remarked: "Whatever Max Liebman decides about 'Your Show of Shows' next season, Imogene Coca doesn't think she'll be with it."*

At the close of the 1952–1953 season in May, there were negotiations and it was decided "Your Show of Shows" would appear three out of every four weeks, with the fourth given over to a rotating "All-Star Revue," headlining Tallulah Bankhead, Martha Raye, and other leading performers. A format change was scheduled for the 1953–1954 season. Judy Johnson, Marguerite Piazza, Mata and Hari, and the Billy Williams Quartette were used less frequently. The Hamilton Trio and the dance team of Bambi Lynn and Rod Alexander were retained but would not be used every week.

The new season opened on September 12, 1953, at the Center Theatre. It began with an introduction by announcer John Cameron Swayze, indicating that the program would present "many new and exciting personalities." This was followed by the cast members "checking in" for the performance. Then Caesar and Coca had a small routine in which she received telegrams wishing her luck on the opening show, while Caesar, playing on his usual insecure persona, worried about receiving none. It all turned out to be a joke on Caesar.

Some of the elements of the show remained familiar. The Hickenloopers and their neighbors were involved in a sketch revolving about a barbecue, with Caesar carried away by outdoor cooking and emerging with barbecue apron, chef's hat, and an enormous side of beef. Caesar performed a solo pantomime as "The Dentist's Apprentice." Coca sang "One

---

* Despite the talk of ending the program, it was still making money for the network. A lead article in *Variety* on February 18, 1953, reported that the show had grossed seven million dollars, "an all-time high in video annals for a single program."

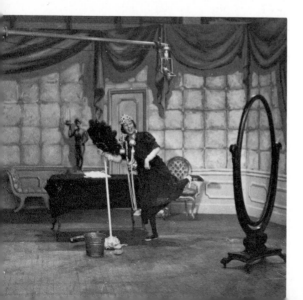

Kiss" as a charwoman at a television station who is momentarily transformed into a grande dame by a string of pearls and a tiara. And the central sketch was an often funny takeoff of the film *From Here to Eternity*, called "From Here to Obscurity." (It was featured in the movie, *Ten From Your Show of Shows*.)

The song-and-dance portions of the show, however, were much more prominent than usual. Guest star Nat "King" Cole sang "A Fool Was I" and Cole Porter's "I Am In Love." Ballerina Tamara Toumanova danced exquisitely to a tango called "The Girl in Satin." And special guest star Lily Pons, in a rare television appearance, not only sang "Je Suis Titania" from *Mignon* but cavorted with Imogene Coca in a spirited rendition of "When Love Goes Wrong," from the film version of the musical *Gentlemen Prefer Blondes*. At one point during the song, the two ladies, dressed in tights and looking astonishingly alike, had a cadenza challenge that not only displayed the beauty of Miss Pons' voice but indicated that Coca could match her, cadenza for cadenza. The show's finale was a song-and-dance number, "Love Never Went to College," featuring singer Robert Monet.

In retrospect, this show seems a likely candidate for enthusiastic notices. But the reviews, on the whole, were not good. The reviewers, in fact, having once put the show on a pedestal, now seemed inclined to throw rocks at it. The New York *Journal-American* called it "curiously unsatisfying," and the *New York Daily News* said that the *From Here to Eternity* satire was "unimaginative and just not funny." The *Washington Times* found the show "considerably uneven, ranging from excellent to pedestrian."

Imogene Coca sings "One Kiss"
and transforms herself from a
charwoman into a grande dame.

Variety was blunt: Max Liebman's decision to change the format was "a mistake. The show is losing its peculiar distinctiveness and falling into the category of vaudeo. . . . The opening segment shaped up as no more than a fair 'Show of Shows' effort."

Though Liebman returned to the original format for the season's second show, the grumbling continued. *Times* columnist Jack Gould, in a September 28 column, wrote: " 'Your Show of Shows' is lacking in real pep or imaginative verve. Perhaps it is the horrendous number of commercials that prevent any continuity or sustained warmth in the show but somehow it has gone cut and dried and impersonal. 'Your Show of Shows' bears the imprint of a production that has had a long run. It needs some first night sparkle and excitement."

The rumors continued through the balance of the year, many of them hinting at bitter arguments among the principals involved. A column emphatically denying these rumors appeared in *Radio Daily*: "Stories to the effect that there has been dissension, conflicts, and philosophical differences between the two stars and their producer are . . . untrue." But despite the "mutual respect and regard" of Caesar, Coca, and Liebman, the future of the program remained in doubt.

In February of 1954, the official closing notice was posted. "Your Show of Shows" would not return after the end of the season. Sid Caesar was going to sign a ten-year contract with NBC, and Imogene Coca was going to do her own half-hour situation comedy. The golden period of "Your Show of Shows" would soon be over.

Immediately and inevitably, the television pundits were expounding on the meaning of it all. Writing in the *World Telegram and Sun*, Harriet Van Horne praised Sid Caesar's growing talents, then added: "I would guess that Mr. Caesar has some dark, unfulfilled places in his heart, some hungers he can't still. Be-

Imogene Coca's most memorable tramp number, "Wrap Your Troubles in Dreams."

cause we live in a world where money is supposed to be the balm for every ill, the first answer that leaps to mind when we're troubled is money." A column by Jack Gould in *The New York Times* reflected on the reason for the show's demise: "What happened? Mr. Caesar and Miss Coca have not lost their technique or artistry. Their performances individually may be just as good as they were four years ago. The difference is that millions of persons now know 'Your Show of Shows' backward and forward. Within its framework there is hardly anything that Mr. Caesar and Miss Coca can do that seems fresh and bright. It is not a case of a viewer not liking the show; he has just seen it before, not once but many times."

Meanwhile, the stars themselves were commenting on the demise of the pro-

gram. In an article by Marie Torre in the *Telegram* (one of a series), Sid Caesar remarked: "The truth is that Max, Coca, and myself have to split up because there just isn't time for the three of us to express ourselves on one show any longer. In other words, we've grown up, and if we hope to continue growing, we must get out on our own. During the past five years, we've done everything that's possible to do within the confines of one show. It's time we were given a chance to express ourselves differently. I know Coca is capable of doing more, and so is Max." He added: "There's been a lot of talk around about Max, Coca and myself breaking up because of friction. That's not true. 'Your Show of Shows' has been a happy road for all of us."

Coca said simply: "It's a sad event. I'm sorry it's happened." But many years later, she noted: "After four years, the ratings were probably getting low—although I can't say for sure. One night I felt I had to get away from everyone, get together with Max and Sid and just talk about things. After a rehearsal, I told them what was happening in my life—people were pushing me to have my own show—and I wanted to know what was happening to them. I told them that if 'Your Show of Shows' was going to die, let us at least be brave about it and present a united front to the press. At the time reporters were calling me up and asking me what my plans were. Sid and Max promised that we would get together the next day. Well, the next day I was rehearsing—dancing away like mad—when David Tebet came up to me. He was very white. He said: 'Coca, you'd better come upstairs.' We walked into a room full of reporters and cameras. That's when I learned 'Your Show of Shows' was dead. I made a fool of myself, crying and carrying on."

For the final show on June 5, 1954, with Faye Emerson (always a welcome visitor) as the guest hostess, some of the most popular sketches and songs were reprised. There was the Hickenlooper sketch in which Doris serves her first meal to Charlie; the French movie "Au Revoir, Ma Cherie or: Toot Toot Tootsie, So Long," and the silent movie about "Bertha, the Sewing-Machine Girl." Caesar, Coca, Reiner, and Morris repeated the sketch in which they play Englishmen attending a soirée given by the Duchess of Twingleman. The Hamilton Trio, with Bill Hayes singing, danced to "Rock the Joint." Hayes sang "Anema E Core," while Pauline Goddard danced.

James Starbuck with look-alikes Imogene Coca and Lily Pons.

A congratulatory kiss from the producer.

Marguerite Piazza sang a medley, and Bambi Lynn and Rod Alexander danced to "Younger Than Springtime." The Billy Williams Quartette rendered "Lazy River" and "Mad About You."

Perhaps the most memorable highlight of this last show was Imogene Coca's performance as the lovable Tramp in "Wrap Your Troubles in Dreams." Here, with James Starbuck, she reprised the Tramp's encounter with a very proper doorman who melts reluctantly before her insouciant charm and good cheer. It was Coca at her best, sweetly poignant, but it was also her final solo turn on "Your Show of Shows." James Starbuck remembers an unscheduled touching moment:

"Coca was supposed to drop ashes in my hand instead of a tip. Instead she flung her arms around me, hugged and kissed me, and burst into tears on stage. I had to stand there with the camera on me. I thought: will that light never go out on that camera? The tears were welling up and starting to run down my face. Everyone who was watching the show started to cry—and there wasn't a dry eye in the house. It was the end of something that was so beautiful."

With the last sketch performed, the last number sung and danced, Faye Emerson spoke the valedictory:

Well, we now come to the finale of "Your Show of Shows"—which is not only the finale of this particular evening but the finale of a great adventure. The show burst upon the television horizon with the image you are about to see. And it is only proper that we close with the now-famous signature, "Stars Over Broadway."

Sid Caesar spoke a few words ("six wonderful years together"), as did Imogene Coca ("the most exciting and thrilling years"), and there was a brief speech by Pat Weaver, now president of NBC. The cast assembled onstage, many of them near tears. The theme song rang throughout the theater. Caesar and Coca tried to smile, but the strain was evident.

"Your Show of Shows" had ended.

Apparently, the critics agreed that the program had been "a great adventure." The many articles following the last show were effusive in their praise and sincere in their regret at the show's departure. The *Variety* reviewer wrote:

The Saturday night extravaganzas possessed those special and peculiar qualities that give them an exclusive niche in the archives of a medium which "Show of Shows" did much to elevate. There had never been before or since the natal day of February 25, 1950, a program that embodied so many show business elements with such skill, imagination and the truly big league touch. . . . The public and the industry are so much indebted to the Liebman-Caesar-Coca trio that it would be graceless and ungrateful not to wish them "all the best" in their individual pursuits.

In an article in the *Philadelphia Inquirer*, Leo Mishkin also saluted the program:

Television is still young enough to make a "farewell appearance" something of an occasion. Especially with a program such as this, a show that instigated and inspired completely new forms and new patterns in the medium, which brought its two stars to a national fame they had never experienced before, and which introduced its producer, Max Liebman, as one of the most imaginative and provocative creators of TV entertainment that the medium has ever developed. Over the course of the last five years, "Your Show of Shows" has almost invariably stood up with the best that TV had to offer, the best, indeed, that any other form of entertainment had to offer as well.

The final show marked the end of a television program that had demonstrated, week after week, that wit and style need not be absent from the small screen. It had shown us that we could laugh at all our foibles and idiosyncrasies without cruelty or self-loathing. It had proven, beyond a shadow of a doubt, that the glories of song and dance could be presented on television without pretentiousness or tedium.

Above all, "Your Show of Shows" demonstrated that, given an extraordinarily talented group of people both in front of and behind the camera, it was possible to turn out ninety minutes of captivating entertainment every week for one hundred and sixty weeks—and to do it *live.*

Virtually all of television is ephemeral. Very few programs remain beacons of light in the gray year-in, year-out world of the all-consuming Tube. "Your Show of Shows" can be included among those few.

A quarter of a century later, the light still glows.

ON
FOLLOWING
PAGE:

*The final curtain call,
June 5, 1954.*

APPENDIX

AWARDS WON BY "YOUR SHOW OF SHOWS"

Academy of Television Arts and Sciences—*"Michael" Award, Best Variety Show, 1950*

Variety—*Special citation to "Your Show of Shows," 1950*

Motion Picture Daily Poll—*Best variety program on TV, 1951*

Look Magazine—*Best Variety Show, 1951*

Sylvania Awards—*Best Variety Show, 1951*

Academy of Television Arts and Sciences—*Best Variety Show, 1951*

Radio Daily Poll of TV Editors—*Best variety show of 1952*

Radio Daily Poll of Radio Critics—*Best variety show of 1952*

TV Digest Popularity Poll—*Favorite Variety-Comedy show for 1952*

Motion Picture Daily Poll—*Best variety program on TV, 1952*

Philadelphia TV Digest—*Favorite variety and comedy show, 1952*

National Association for Better Radio and TV—*Best Variety Program, 1953*

Motion Picture Daily "Fame" Award—*Best variety show, best network program, best comedy show*

Saturday Review of Literature Poll—*Top show on TV*

Radio TV Mirror—*Favorite variety program*

TV Radio Life—*Distinguished Achievement award*

TV Guide Gold Medal Award—*Best variety show*

American Weekly Annual TV Poll—*Best variety program for two years*